"George has 'Mumfied' the teams I've coached over the past twenty years. He has a style of mindfulness that goes beyond 'just sitting/breathing' to focusing while in action. For anyone needing to perform at the highest level, this book is for you."

—PHIL JACKSON, thirteen-time NBA champion and President of the New York Knicks

"Proper mental preparation can be the difference between average and good, or very good and great. George is able to help make that difference."

—Al Skinner, Jr., former coach, Boston College Eagles men's basketball 1997–2010

"Working with George in my college years was a turning point in my career as an athlete and in my life. Our many discussions, his advice, and his support helped me become confident in myself. Because of him, I am the player and person that I am today."

—Laura Georges, France women's international soccer team

"George steadily kept me mentally ready for games, building my self-confidence and keeping me calm and relaxed via self-talk exercises and weekly meetings."

—Reggie Jackson, point guard, Detroit Pistons

"George has been able to help me think about the sport of basketball from a different perspective. He has shown me everything isn't physical; a lot of it is mental, including self-talk. Being able to use self-talk as a self-motivation aid is something I put into practice every day."

—Wayne Selden, Jr., guard, Jayhawks, Kansas University NBA prospect

"George has been the most significant teacher I have had in body, mind, and spirit. He opened doors for me that forever changed my perception of the 'game.' I have never met a being more present, or who responds more intelligently in the present moment. He is a true teacher; one who shares, guides, and will lead you to uncover your own power to elevate your game both on and off the court. He's the type of teacher that you go back to years later to say, 'thank you.'"

—Nancy Legan, former captain, Boston College Eagles women's volleyball

"Understanding why I was doing something, how to achieve that goal, and approaching the task from a clear, stable mental, emotional, and physical standpoint is what George helped me to achieve. This provided purity in the process, whether outcomes were good or bad, and enabled me to accept the outcomes knowing that I put my mind, body, and soul into achieving my goal."

—**Kyle Casey,** former co-captain, Harvard Crimson men's basketball

"George has helped me realize that the mental side of athletics is just as—if not more—important than the physical aspect of the game. By focusing on the mental aspect of the game, it will help improve my physical result."

—**Zach Auguste,** Notre Dame Fighting Irish forward, NBA prospect

"George did a tremendous job of teaching our players and staff that being mentally prepared is just as important as being physically prepared. He also taught us the importance of staying 'mentally present' which allows you to be your best in the moment that you are in."

—**Milan Brown,** coach, The College of the Holy Cross Crusaders men's basketball

"George has helped me become a better me! His wisdom on being a mindful athlete stems from the core of who and what mindfulness looks like in its greatest form. *The Mindful Athlete* will change what it means to be an athlete forever!"

—**Steven Hailey,** former point guard, Boston College Eagles men's basketball

"Working with George has allowed me to develop mindfulness of my body and my surroundings. That has not only improved my play on the field but has helped me develop as a person and uncover the characteristics that I want to be and express in my life."

—**Max Breiter,** high school soccer player

"I told George once, it seems like playing goalie is all mental. He laughed and said everything is mental. Teaching me how to play the mental game, George has helped me unlock conscious performance."

—**Henry Donnellan,** high school lacrosse player

"George Mumford has tremendous knowledge and experience in sports psychology that helps players and teams perform at peak potential. Every athlete has highs and lows throughout their careers. George helped me gain perspective and change my outlook when I was in a rut and I emerged as a better player, leader, and person. I am honored to have worked with George and I know others can learn from the insight he shares."

—Kia McNeill, assistant coach, Northeastern University Huskies women's soccer

"A truly valuable, unique, and inspiring door into the cultivation of mind-body unity and purpose. George's love of basketball and of life comes through on every page and shapes his remarkable story and the enormous impact he has had at the highest levels of The Game. But George's real message here is that *anybody* can cultivate mindfulness through ongoing practice, fine-tune his or her way of being, and thus, take care of what most needs taking care of and do what most needs to be done."

—Jon Kabat-Zinn, founder of Mindfulness-Based Stress Reduction (MBSR), *Full Catastrophe Living* and *Mindfulness for Beginners*

"Full of wisdom and heart—both a moving story and powerful practices from a very fine teacher—George Mumford shows how to find freedom in a game fully played and a life well lived."

—Jack Kornfield, *A Path with Heart*

"George Mumford has written a fantastic book—inspiring, funny, and insightful. I'm amongst the people who have urged George for years to write a book, and I couldn't be happier for him, and all of us who get to read it and reread it. Qualities like mindfulness, concentration, trust, and the forging of a team spirit really come alive."

—Sharon Salzberg, *Real Happiness* and *Real Happiness at Work*

"George Mumford's insight into mindful performance has helped many world-class athletes reach their true and full potential. This engaging book will help you to lower your stress level and raise the bar in your own game and life."

—Jim Afremow, PhD, *The Champion's Mind*

THE MINDFUL ATHLETE

THE MINDFUL ATHLETE

SECRETS TO PURE PERFORMANCE

GEORGE MUMFORD

 PARALLAX PRESS

BERKELEY, CALIFORNIA

Parallax Press
P.O. Box 7355
Berkeley, CA
94707
parallax.org

Parallax Press is the publishing division of
Plum Village Community of Engaged Buddhism, Inc.

Cover and text design by Josh Michels
Cover image © EvgeniyQ by iStock/Getty Images
Author photo © Nancy Carbonaro

ISBN: 978-1-941529-25-6 (paperback)

Data for hardback:
Library of Congress Cataloging-in-Publication Data
Mumford, George.
 The mindful athlete : secrets to pure performance / George Mumford ; foreword by
Phil Jackson.
   pages cm
 ISBN 978-1-941529-06-5 (hardback)
1. Sports--Psychological aspects. 2. Athletes--Psychology. 3. Success--Psychologi-
cal aspects. I. Title.
 GV706.4.M83 2015
 796.01'9--dc23
                         2015009380

6 7 8 / 22 21 20

May all beings
experience excellence
and wisdom with
grace and ease.

CONTENTS

INTRODUCTION TO THE PAPERBACK EDITION

Since writing *The Mindful Athlete*, I've met mindful athletes from across the country of every shape, size, color, and age. Whether we know it or not, we are all mindful athletes.

Life is a marathon. We go and go, others running alongside us. In order to run this marathon, we need to train in the same way any other athlete trains to compete effectively in a sport. Without awareness and clear intention, we may start off too slowly, not finishing the race in a timely and respectable manner. Without diligence and practice, we may go too quickly, burning out before we're able to get what we want and becoming disabled or quitting before we make it to the finish line.

Our challenge and our opportunity is to mindfully train so we find our own optimum pace. That pace is the place where we are able to notice and navigate what is currently in front of us and at the same time be open to learning and exploring what comes next.

My hope is that the exercises and ideas in *The Mindful Athlete* help you move forward with ease and curiosity. It is that sweet spot of relaxed readiness that I've found leads to peak learning and performance. Noticing, finding, and cultivating that sweet spot will help you succeed in whatever field you're playing on in this dynamic ever-changing world.

FOREWORD:
PHIL JACKSON

Over twenty years ago, I asked George Mumford to come and teach our players the skill of mindfulness. George had been recommended by Jon Kabat-Zinn as a teacher who would fit in well with our players because he knew mindfulness, and he had played basketball and attended the University of Massachusetts back in the day of Al Skinner and Dr. J, so we knew he understood the game. George came and we hit it off. Our relationship blossomed and now we are working together again in the NBA and he has written this wonderful book.

I had tried using meditation with my Chicago Bulls teams during the early nineties. We had been successful as a team and I believed they had the ability to focus on and accomplish whatever tasks were put in front of them. The next group of players that we brought in with the team didn't have Michael Jordan as a leader and we needed some way to practice focus and concentration, as well as deal with stress, and develop our ability to work together as a team. I thought the team's training in mindfulness should fall on the shoulders of George as our meditation teacher rather than on me as their coach.

We had played one season without Jordan and we'd done quite well. However, ten of the twelve players were holdovers from our three-peat championship teams of the early nineties. They had bonded and were seasoned. Our newest group was trying to find that bond. We experimented with quite a few things that season. Instead of the usual two-a-day practices in training camp, for example, we were using a shortened version of conditioning in the morning, taking a break for lunch and implementing some mental training, and then going back on the court for a full practice. This made for a six-hour day. It wasn't easy for the players to adapt to this structure, but George taught mental training exercises that really helped us stay fresh and on track.

Things took off later that season when Michael came back to League and the Bulls. Successes followed over the next three season championships. During this time, the Bulls had a number of players who were in their late twenties, were parents, and were quite mature. This was a good balance because we also had Dennis Rodman and other players with strong personalities in the mix. One day the players all came out to practice wearing T-shirts that had a cartoon image of the team sleeping during meditation. The shirt showed a bunch of zzzz's coming out of their heads with the inscription: "Getting Mumfied." George provided great leadership during that period and I think he gained insight into the mindset of the professional athlete, the attention span athletes had available, and how mindfulness can bear fruit in that context.

Next stop for George and me was Los Angeles and the Lakers. George, who has always lived in Massachusetts, had to fly cross-country regularly to come to California to work with our guys. This was a team that had done reasonably well during the regular season the past two years, but had been swept out of the playoffs in embarrassing style. George had his work cut out for him. With his clarity, humor, and deep knowledge of mindfulness practice, he was able to reach this crew. We set up our video room with theater style chairs and George would come in the room and get them to sit on the edge of their seats, assume a relaxed and upright position so they could practice conscious breathing, and he would have them focus on just being right where they were, fully in the present moment.

Fast forward two years to 2002 and our third attempt to win a title and repeat what had happened at previous Bulls championships. The Sacramento Kings fiercely challenged us that year. The series dragged into the seventh game on the Kings' court. The morning of the final game we had an 11:00 a.m. buffet for a 3:00 p.m. game, with video for the players before the buffet. My coaching staff and I had met at 9:30 that morning in the hotel café to make sure we had covered all our points before we were to meet with our guys. When we made it to our banquet room, five minutes ahead of schedule, every player was already in his spot ready to sit and breathe together. As the game went into overtime that afternoon, the team stayed steady with the same collected calm they had shown before brunch.

A lot of athletes think the trick to getting better is just to work harder. But there is a great power in non-action and non-thinking. The hardest thing, after all the work and all the time spent on training and technique, is just being fully present in the moment. Time after time, team after team, I have seen athletes transform and have seen championships saved by players who believed in Mumford's one-mind, one-breath efforts.

INTRODUCTION:
THE ZONE

Seventy-two million people were watching game six of the 1998 NBA Championship Finals between the Chicago Bulls and the Utah Jazz. With only eighteen seconds left in the game and the Jazz ahead by one point, an invisible shift seemed to occur: Michael Jordan stripped the ball from Karl Malone, slipped away from Bryon Russell so deftly that Russell careened to the floor, and effortlessly made the winning shot with only five seconds to spare, bringing the Bulls to their sixth championship and second three-peat. It would be Michael Jordan's and Phil Jackson's last game with the Bulls, and it is considered one of the greatest plays in NBA sports history. Fans remember what they were doing at that moment the way some people remember where they were when JFK was shot or Neil Armstrong landed on the moon. If you're too young to remember those milestones, fill in the blanks as you see fit.

Life is available only in the present moment.[1]

—THICH NHAT HANH

I was sitting a few rows behind the bench, watching this groundbreaking play unfold, knowing that Michael was in that very special place called the Zone. "When I got that rebound, my thoughts were very positive," Michael recounted later. "The crowd gets quiet, and the moment starts to become the moment for me. That's what we've been trying to do...that's part of that Zen Buddhism stuff. Once you get into the moment, you know when you are there. Things start to move slowly, you start to see the court very well. You start reading what the defense is trying to do. I saw that moment. When I saw that moment and the opportunity to take advantage of it… I never doubted myself. I never doubted the whole game. We were hanging too close."

I'd been doing "that Zen Buddhism stuff" with the Bulls for five years when Michael Jordan made that famous play, and I had seen countless athletes experience the Zone. By that time, I'd also taught mindfulness to people in every walk of life, from the locker room to the boardroom, from Yale to jail.

Back in the day when I embarked on the journey that would lead me here, people didn't use the word "mindfulness." It was called stress management, of which I had plenty—stress, that is. And it was during a moment of extreme stress—crisis, really—that Phil Jackson contacted me in 1993. The Bulls had just come out of that three-peat when the team fell into a crisis: Jordan had announced his retirement in the wake of his father's murder. Media attention on Jordan, intense under normal circumstances, had reached an almost frenzied state. Meanwhile, the team's identity was adrift; it had been so wrapped up in Jordan that they were referred to as the Jordan Airs. Without their superstar, public perception of the Bulls' ability to keep their stride hit an all-time low; team morale went south for the ride. In the midst of this adversity, with team members in various states of emotional distress, Phil had to rebuild a team and bring harmony to discord. That's when he reached out and brought me to his training camp to teach mindfulness and help heal the team.

At the time, I was a full-time staff member at the Center for Mindfulness (formerly called the Stress Reduction and Relaxation Program) in Shrewsbury, Massachusetts, and I was teaching mindfulness to prison inmates in a program I helped develop with Jon Kabat-Zinn in the early nineties. Over the course of five years we'd taught mindfulness to over five thousand inmates in five different locations. I had never been incarcerated, but in addition to being familiar with the stress experienced by professional athletes, I could understand the stress experienced by some of these inmates because, like many of them, I grew up in the inner city where impulse control is, shall we say, something of a problem.

When Michelangelo was asked how he created his masterpieces, he replied that all he did was to chip away to get to the masterpiece that was already inside. I believe we're all chipping away to get to that masterpiece, even those of us who grew up in the ghetto, on the wrong side of the tracks. We all have a divine spark within us, but we've either crushed it, created an ingenious system for hiding out, or devised ways of being that make us feel separate. I now regard each person I meet as a caterpillar in a chrysalis. In order to become butterflies, we have to break our way into freedom and transformation. Mindfulness is a tool we can use to do this in the most skillful way. Admittedly, I had to hit rock bottom with my ass on fire before I figured out the most skillful way out of my *own* chrysalis.

Mindfulness was the skillful means to help me emerge, and I have used mindfulness techniques to help athletes of every shape, size, age, gender, and skill level emerge to be their own selves. Mindfulness comes out of Buddhist meditation, an ancient practice with many layers of complexity. What I offer in this book is a synthesis of mindfulness principles that fall under the aegis of what I call the Five Spiritual Superpowers. These Superpowers are my personal spin on the Buddha's Eightfold Path and on his teaching of the Five Spiritual Faculties: faith, diligence, mindfulness, concentration, and insight. The Eightfold Path was the Buddha's understanding of the way out of suffering. In his book *Old Path White Clouds*, the Zen teacher Thich Nhat Hanh tells the story of the way the Buddha regarded the Eightfold Path and all his teachings. According to the story, the Buddha said, "My teaching is not a dogma or a doctrine." He goes on, "I must state clearly that my teaching is a method to experience reality and is not reality itself, just as a finger pointing at the moon is not the moon itself." [2]

Consider these Superpowers to be like spokes in a wheel: They are nonlinear and they work together. Take one away, and the wheel doesn't turn. Remove the hub or the center, and you have no wheel. Purists interested in a more traditional approach will find many books on the subject of mindfulness, several written by my friends and esteemed colleagues. At the end of this book I've collected a list of these that have been most influential to me.

ASS ON FIRE: THE FIVE SPIRITUAL SUPERPOWERS

CHAPTER 1

Pain brought me to mindfulness, not any desire to reach nirvana or pop out of any chrysalis. It was "unlearning" certain habits and thought patterns hard-wired in my brain and walking through my pain, rather than avoiding it, that ultimately put me on a joyful journey of self-discovery. I grew up in Dorchester, Boston, in the fifties and sixties. Here's how the Urban Dictionary defines the place: "A ghetto in Boston where hood rats and thugs kill each other over basketball courts, street corners, and anything else they feel like. Most people know to steer clear of this area and let the ghetto rats cull themselves out of existence." Here's another definition of my hometown you'll read on that site: "When walking down Blue Hill, bring a Kevlar helmet and vest."

I did not live far from Blue Hill Avenue. You get the picture.

I was number ten in a family of thirteen children. I had seven older sisters, which means that I had eight mothers. These eight mothers took care of me when I got hurt, which was often, since I came into this world accident-prone: I was always hitting my head on oven doors, getting stepped on, and knocked around. If lightning was going to strike, it would strike me. I've come to realize that stress itself can create a vulnerability to being injury-prone; no doubt I grew up internalizing the stress of my family. That's how the mind-body connection works.

Of course, no one knew that back then. We just tried to get by—barely—living from paycheck to paycheck. Sometimes the electricity got turned off because we couldn't pay the bill. Other times we had no heat because we couldn't afford heating oil. There were even times when we couldn't go to school because there wasn't enough money for bread or school lunches.

My parents did the best they could, all things considered. My mother was an elevator operator in a hotel. My father was a laborer on the New Haven Railroad by day and a barber by night. They both came from a line of Alabama sharecroppers who worked all year under the crack of a whip for twenty bucks. Alcoholism was one way they dealt with their pain, and my father carried on that lineage. He was raged on at the railroad, and he raged on us when he came home. No one was spared, not even the family dog.

Basically, you did not mess with my father or engage in acts of self-expression unless you wanted serious trouble. I will never forget the day my sister was getting married and I asked him to give me a quo vadis haircut. He was so outraged by what he thought was a radical request that he shaved me completely bald. I attended that wedding in a veil of humiliation and anger.

I learned early to keep my mouth shut. It has taken me decades to unlearn it.

When my dad wasn't railing on me for no good reason, the cops or others were doing so. I recall getting pulled over by the police while riding in the back seat of a friend's car. When I asked, "What's the violation, officer?" the police officer responded, "Who the fuck are you—Perry Mason?" I had to be silent or else I would have been beaten into submission.

This, I believe,
is the great Western truth:
that each of us is a completely
unique creature and that,
if we are ever to give any gift
to the world, it will have
to come out of our own
experience and fulfillment
of our own potentialities,
not someone else's. [3]

—JOSEPH CAMPBELL

Being African American I had two choices: speak up and get beat up (and often go to jail) or be quiet. Be very quiet. I chose the latter option, which became woven into my emotional blueprint: I did not speak up to my father, to cops, or even to coaches. I learned to shut up and be, and I carried that oppression around like an albatross. Whatever emotional pain I experienced, I unconsciously buried in my body. No wonder pain became my constant companion.

Looking back now, maybe my dad thought that by literally trying to knock the spirit out of me, he was protecting me from the perils of free thinking. This was the United States of America in the midst of the sixties counterculture, after all. As fate would have it, Martin Luther King, Jr., used to preach in a church down the street from our house. His freedom marches and the civil rights movement were part of the social fabric of my youth. There was also the birth of rock and roll, the sexual revolution, feminism, peace protests, Vietnam, and the so-called dawning of the Age of Aquarius that lit the stage for the human potential movement. The Esalen Institute in California, and later the Omega Institute in New York, both still thriving today, were beacons of this movement, bookending the country as spiritual centers dedicated to personal transformation, well-being, and consciousness-raising.

Never in my wildest dreams would I have imagined that decades later I'd be teaching at the Omega Institute myself. In those days, nobody in Dorchester focused on consciousnessraising. That word wasn't even in our vocabulary. We focused on survival. As the sixties unfolded in a whirlwind of experimentation and turmoil, I found my nirvana in basketball, music, and drugs.

OPEN YOUR FUNKY MIND

I had always played sports in the streets—dodgeball, stickball, baseball, football, and tag. Like millions of inner-city youth, I had NBA dreams from a young age. Sport was a salvation and a way out of the ghetto. I loved the Celtics, the Red Sox, the Lakers, Jerry West, and Elgin Baylor, among many others. They fed my dreams when, at four feet eleven inches tall, I went to middle school, dribbling with confidence and working on different shooting styles until I perfected a two-handed push shot. I suddenly shot up to five feet eleven inches in high school and my feet became a vortex of growing pains.

My injury-proneness was just about to escalate to new heights.

I used to play with ten-pound weights on each ankle until one day when I went up high to take a shot during a game and landed awkwardly, spraining both of them. From then on I played with both of my ankles taped up. My knees were stiff and ached constantly. In the spring of my junior year, something popped in my knee. Undaunted, I kept playing until my muscle atrophied, my leg became too weak to run or jump on, and I tore a patellar tendon in my left knee.

I was injured so often in my youth that I was in crutches every year throughout high school, and I had such intense back pain that I had to sleep on a bed board. I kept my NBA dreams going, however, until their death knell came when my coach sent me to an orthopedic specialist and I got the coach in trouble when that specialist billed the high school for his services. My coach rarely put me in games again for fear I'd get hurt; instead, he urged me to become an accountant. One day, after not getting to play at all, I quit the team. I returned the next day, hoping basketball would provide a path to college and a way out. I ended up going to the University of Massachusetts on an academic scholarship, with pain as my mascot. But by then, I'd picked up a few vices along the way.

No one told me when I was growing up that I could alter my consciousness by going within. Even at church, no one helped me stay in touch with the spark of divinity once I left the pew. I had no real spiritual foundation, though I longed for spirit. I found it first in John Barleycorn—I was given my first taste of beer at about the same time I learned to walk. I liked that enough to move on to more sophisticated spirits, like my father's Seagram's 7 whiskey that I enjoyed in private. At an early age, I found God in getting high and leaving my body, floating into space, and taking off—anything that would get me away from the experience of physical and emotional pain was welcome.

I floated further into space in my teens when a group of kids I'd met at a YMCA turned me on to heroin. We called it "skag" because it was inferior to white boys' heroin. We'd sniff it off the end of nail files and go on about our business. On heroin my pain lifted and my spirits soared even higher. I could suddenly speak out and be gregarious without fear. Jimi Hendrix had hit the charts in those days, and I could relate to having "purple haze all in my brain." Music, in fact, was another form of bliss that got me high, transporting me far away to some Shangri-la of the mind. I recall listening to groups like Funkadelic, whose psychedelic lyrics to "Free Your Mind and Your Ass Will Follow" spoke to a generation of spirit-seeking junkies: "Open up your funky mind and you can fly/Free your mind and your ass will follow/ The kingdom of heaven is within."

I had yet to find that kingdom of heaven within, but I'd certainly found my little helper.

There were a lot of ironies around my drug use back then. One of them was that during a hospital visit for chronic back pain, I was given Darvon, a powerful pain-killing narcotic. That one little pill packed with white crystalline powder not only relieved my pain, it got me an even more agreeable high than skag. Under the influence of Darvon, the kingdom of heaven felt very near. I was even more outgoing and freer to speak out. It had taken a formal check-in with the medical establishment to tip the scales, but there I was: I had become a bonafide substance abuser.

I had no idea that in taking this path, I was robbing myself of the stress hardiness people develop naturally in life. And my descent into drug use didn't follow the traditional trajectory from smoking cigarettes, to smoking pot, and progressing onward. I avoided pot because I'd been told that it stunted your physical growth. I wanted every possibility to grow tall. So instead I went straight to heroin and stunted my emotional growth. Call that junkie wisdom.

DOUBLE LIFE

As my drug use became more routine, particularly after high school, I developed a very well-fortified internal firewall that kept two parts of my life separate: I was Joe College during the day, and a member of Kool and the Gang at night. Determined that the two should never meet, I also forged an uncanny ability to maintain a double life. That firewall would eventually become my Great Wall of Pain and that double life would be my undoing, but at the time I had no idea.

Sports remained a huge part of my life throughout college, when I had the good fortune of rooming at the University of

Massachusetts with Dr. J, aka Julius Erving. Dr. J was indisputably the Michael Jordan of his time and would eventually be inducted into the NBA Hall of Fame. But back then we were all just college kids with NBA dreams.

> *We emerge into the light*
> *not by denying our pain, but*
> *by walking out through it.*[4]

—JOAN BORYSENKO

The first time I met Dr. J, he was playing basketball with dress shoes on. My first reaction to this sight was: Who is this wiry homey playing basketball and dunking on people in dress shoes? My second thought was: Wow, this dude can play. He had great control of his body, could dribble and pass like a guard, jump and rebound like a center, float in the air like a butterfly, and sting like a bee with quick and precise movements that finished in the basket. Everyone was in awe of his physical prowess and agility. He could maneuver in street shoes even while injured or under duress. He could dunk two balls at once with his large hands and excellent hand-eye coordination.

Even when J had injured his ankle and could barely walk without limping, he played and dunked on people with grace and ease. Ditto the time he broke his big toe. He just went out anyhow, despite his pain, and played with focus and intention. This was a supreme example of self-efficacy (more on that later).

I didn't realize it at the time, but J was a natural born mindful athlete who played the "inner game" before the term was coined. He was always in flow and living fully in the present moment, responding and adapting to what was happening around him rather than reacting and fighting against it. He seemed to let situations speak to him; he observed and learned. He was always upbeat, supportive, encouraging, kind, and generous—important wholesome qualities for the mindful athlete to develop in order to flourish—yet he held others accountable without making them wrong. He never complained about going to practice, being in pain, or being depressed when he played badly or lost a game. He seemed happy to be alive.

I also don't remember anyone running set plays for J or featuring his talents. He was all about "we," not "me." He loved playing basketball and developing the craft, and didn't complain about other players *not* being able to dunk or run, or about not having other like-minded people on the team with

him. Dr. J was the only person of color on both the JV and var-
sity teams. I would have liked to stay by his side after college
but eventually we parted ways. After his junior year, Dr. J went
pro. I simply went professional.

WORKING FOR THE LIFE

On the advice of a coach, I put my passion for sports on the
back burner and studied finance in college. I went through the
motions and did what I needed in order to do okay at finance,
but my heart and mind weren't in it. In my mind, I was still
playing basketball.

By that time, my heroin use had really taken off: I'd gone
from sniffing, to skin popping, to mainlining, and my firewall
was stronger than ever. I ended up working as a financial analyst for a company that made sophisticated communications
and guidance systems for space shuttles, cruise missiles, and
nuclear-powered submarines. I had security clearance on my
badge and track marks on my forearm. I always made sure to
wear long sleeves.

I was married for two years and we were together for
nine years. We met in the summer of 1969, got married in
1975, separated in 1977, and the divorce was final in 1978.
The divorce was devastating to me and it was one more sign
that my life was falling apart. But I kept up a front at work,

because being married gave me carte blanche to be late; it made me seem "normal." There was a lot of shame associated with divorce at that time as well, never mind all my other shame-inducing behaviors. Though I managed finances at work, my personal house of finance was a mess. I spent money recklessly on drugs and eventually ruined my credit. I lost my car. To make sure that no one knew about it, I woke up at the crack of dawn, took public transportation to work, and got there early enough to leave by 4:00 p.m. so no one would see me get back on the bus—to my mother's house. I'd get dope sick if I didn't get high a couple times a day.

In fact, it was probably *because* I got high so often that I was able to maintain this crazy double life, pushing around my repressed emotional weight like Sisyphus with his boulder. Even when a needle broke off in my arm while I was getting high, I thought I was invincible. I didn't even believe the doctors in the emergency room who told me that if I didn't change my life, I would die. It wasn't until 1984, when I was walking around with a high fever and a severe staph infection that landed me in the emergency room again, that I realized how close to death I was. But yet again, the doctor gave me painkillers when he released me from the hospital; this time, it was the narcotic Percocet. You'd think doctors would understand that giving narcotics to an addict is like giving candy to a kid, but who was I to protest? I ended up selling the Percocet to buy more drugs.

The following month, on April 1, a friend who I hadn't seen in a long time popped into my life out of the blue. He'd been a longtime substance abuser like me but had gotten solidly clean and sober through the Twelve-Step AA program. That day he insisted I go to an AA meeting with him. I agreed on a whim, but found the meeting was no April Fools' Day joke.

The only way out is always through.[5]

—ROBERT FROST

By then I was not only sick and tired of being sick and tired; I was more like the walking dead. A refrain in Janis Joplin's song "Me and Bobby McGee" perfectly described that moment: *Freedom's just another word for nothing left to lose.* That's where I was; I had nothing to lose because I'd already lost everything. In a strange, messed-up way, I was free—free to start over from scratch, free to let down my guard and ask for help, free to step out of my comfort zones and take risks in an effort to reinvent myself—because the alternative was to die. The renowned spiritual teacher J. Krishnamurti said that freedom is now or never. I chose now.

THE WAY OUT IS THE WAY IN

I don't know why it often takes a crisis or a fastball from the universe knocking us off our feet for us to finally have our ass on fire enough to act. Maybe it's a flaw in the human condition, or maybe it's simply *part of* the human condition. In any case, the gift of desperation compels us to move forward. Without fire in our lives, we sometimes don't have the internal combustion necessary to change and take risks. We get too comfortable being comfortable—even if we're mired in the comfort of mediocrity or worse. We just don't move our ass. I'll get more into motivation later on.

During this time in my life, I slowly came to understand how having your ass on fire—or what I call AOF—not only moves us human beings into action, but compels us to seek our truths and act with conviction in life. This pertains as much to mindful athletes as it does to anyone else. I know this for a fact because I've lived it, and I've had the good fortune to help many other people live it over the years, both on and off the courts.

During that first AA meeting—and despite my initial

resistance—it was impossible to ignore the wisdom in those Twelve Steps. Step one was easy, in any case: 1. Admitting that I was powerless over alcohol and drugs, and that my life had become unmanageable as a result. Steps two, three, and four sounded pretty reasonable too: 2. Believing that a Power greater than myself could restore me to sanity (which I knew did not take me off the hook). 3. Making a decision to turn my life over to the care of God *as I understood Him* (or Her, or It), meaning that I did not have to subscribe to any organized religion or to a traditional God, and that I was free to believe in anything I wanted—the point was to believe. 4. Making a searching and fearless moral inventory of myself—a pretty big job, since I had quite a backlog of emotional inventory in my personal warehouse.

You have to begin somewhere. As Pema Chödrön puts it in her book *The Places That Scare You*, "Right here is a good place to start. Start where you are."[6] This is true in life and in sports: There might not ever be a "right" time to start. In fact, often what prevents people from moving forward is the daunting sense that they'll never get where they intend to go, so why bother even starting? But as many of us know, taking small steps, consistently, in the right direction will eventually yield big results. This is one of the most simple and profound truths in life. You have to start taking baby steps, even though you know you'll fall down. If you don't begin the process—and you don't fall down a lot—you'll never walk.

So I got out of my own macho way, let my guard down completely, and began my own process. I reached out for help and began to build a community of support around me: a therapist, various support groups, a free inpatient detox program where I could be anonymous. I knew that it would be much harder to recover if I was unemployed, so I did whatever it took to keep my job and my sanity intact. But without the veil of drink and drug masking my pain, it all came rushing back: the intense chronic lower back pain, the migraines, the craving for short-term relief that I'd appeased with substance abuse for years. There were days when it was so intensely difficult to stay sober that I had to step into the men's room at work, close a stall door, get on my knees, and recite the serenity prayer to myself: *God grant me the serenity to accept the things I cannot change, the courage to change the things I can, and the wisdom to know the difference.* Even though I recited this prayer often, I never thought I'd really see the day when it would feel real to me and be more than just words I said to get through the hard stuff.

But somehow things started to shift. One day a psychotherapist referred me to a stress management program offered by my company's HMO. This was back when stress management was the term used for mindfulness. The program introduced me to techniques for managing chronic pain that included meditation and yoga. It was a slow but powerful revelation. I learned to listen to my body. When my backaches occurred, I understood that it was a sign that I was under too much stress and needed to investigate my pain. I began to look for its cause, treat it gently, and adapt my behaviors to take care of it rather than hide it. In essence, I began to figure it out. When I felt a migraine coming on, I would lie down and do deep breathing, visualizing the oxygen moving through the regions where the tightness was, creating space in my head, and allowing the tightness to flow out with my out-breath. I learned how to be in the moment, slow things down, practice bare awareness, and listen to my body. Invariably, my body told me what it needed.

SITTING STILL

I had the good fortune of being in the right place at the right time and learning from some of the finest mavericks in the field: Joan Borysenko, Larry Rosenberg, Jon Kabat-Zinn, and Sharon Salzberg. Even so, the first time I tried to meditate, it would have been easier to bench-press fifty-pound weights than sit still. I went to my first sitting meditation retreat back in the day when it was not common for African Americans to meditate with predominantly white people in a small New

England town. When I was told to buy a cushion for meditating, I went out and bought an actual sofa cushion; that's how clueless I was.

Just sitting for any length of time was painful. I had no flexibility in my body and could not get comfortable no matter how hard I tried. (I didn't realize at the time that I was actually trying *too hard*—but more on that later as well.) My knees and ankles hurt. My back ached. I kept moving around from the cushion to a chair and back again, no doubt distracting the meditators around me. My body just didn't want to sit still. And then there was my mind, flitting around and wandering, fixating on sensations, anxieties, and cravings that came up. But the practice of mindfulness, as I'll address in these pages, slowly taught me how to work through this.

I began learning Insight Meditation and I started a daily mindfulness practice after completing a twenty-one-day detox program in 1984. I committed to a regular practice and, a few years later, I discovered the Cambridge Insight Meditation Center (CIMC), where I continued to practice.

By then I'd been clean for several years but I still had a double life going—a double life of an entirely different nature. My deep commitment to meditation and mindfulness was in stark contrast to my daily life as a financial analyst. The former filled me with a sense of purpose and joy, while the latter was a dead, soul-crushing experience. I wanted to cut this cord and be truly free—but how? I had no alternative job, no backup plan, and little security. Still, I decided to focus more on *what* I wanted, versus *how* I was going to get it.

By coincidence, right around this time, in 1988, the mythologist and philosopher Joseph Campbell appeared in a six-part television documentary series called *The Power of Myth*. The series was based on interviews between Campbell and journalist Bill Moyers. The interviews were also published as a book with the same title. Filmed at George Lucas's Skywalker Ranch, the documentary was an exploration of Campbell's sweeping work chronicling how myths have shaped our culture and consciousness throughout the ages.

At one point during this widely watched documentary, Moyers asked Campbell if Campbell ever felt, in what seemed from the outside to be a charmed life, as if he was helped in his journey of self-discovery by "hidden hands." Campbell replied, "All the time. It is miraculous. I even have a superstition that has grown on me as a result of invisible hands coming all the time—namely, that if you do follow your bliss you put yourself on a kind of track that has been there all the while, waiting for you, and the life that you ought to be living is the one you are living. When you can see that, you begin to meet people who are in your field of bliss, and they open doors to you. I say, follow your bliss and don't be afraid, and doors will open where you didn't know they were going to be."[7]

Joseph Campbell probably had no idea that those three words—"follow your bliss"—would so deeply resonate with viewers that they'd become an enduring cultural trope that still inspires people today to take leaps of faith. In fact, at that time my life was already affirming the words of Joseph Campbell; I'd already shifted my focus to my "field of bliss" and started meeting people who opened doors for me. And then one day instead of going to work, I took a mental health day and went to my weekly interview with Larry Rosenberg, who was my meditation teacher at the time. Larry took one look at me and said: "What's going on with you today? You look pretty happy." He didn't miss a beat when I told him that I'd simply decided not to go to work. "You should make a habit of that," he replied. So I did.

Shortly thereafter, I gave notice to my boss, packed up my things, and told my coworkers about my decision to leave. Nearly every one of them, all pretty miserable at the job, said to me in earnest, "I wish I could do that." Of course, they *could* have done that; they could have shifted their focus to their own fields of bliss. Maybe their asses weren't on fire enough, or maybe they just didn't believe there was a way out. The author Anne Lamott once wrote about a sermon in which the pastor said that if you put bees in a glass jar, they wouldn't fly out. Lamott wrote, "...they'll walk around on the glass floor, imprisoned by the glass surrounding them, when all they'd have to do is look up and they could fly away."

No one had specifically told me that all I had to do was look up, but in essence that's what I did. I finally opened up my funky mind in the right way and realized that I could fly. I took off and never looked back.

FULL CIRCLE

I'm not sure that I would have been able to make that leap of faith without having committed by then to a spiritual practice. In 1986 I went back to school and received a Master of Education in Counseling Psychology from Cambridge College in Cambridge, Massachusetts. For two years after that, I didn't work and lived off what little savings I'd accrued. I committed myself to reading almost every book I could find on the subjects of mindfulness, metaphysics, psychology, and philosophy. I was basically trying to figure out what I wanted to be when I grew up, while attending regular silent retreats, sittings, talks, and teachings at the Insight Meditation Society (IMS) in Barre, Massachusetts, and at the Cambridge Insight Meditation Center (CIMC).

With time I became a practice leader, responding to

requests at the Center for meditation instruction. By 1989 I was living at CIMC as a resident and I stayed on there for many years, participating in teacher training and doing my first Mindfulness-Based Stress Reduction and Relaxation internship with Jon Kabat-Zinn. That parlayed into more work and study at the Stress Reduction and Relaxation Program (SRRP) at the University of Massachusetts Medical Center, where I became a program director and then a member of the Board of Directors of IMS, CIMC, and the Spirit Rock Meditation Center, an Insight Meditation practice center in Woodacre, California.

It was during this period, around 1991, that Jon Kabat-Zinn and I worked together to open up an inner-city satellite clinic in Worcester, Massachusetts. I later became a full-time staff member at SRRP (which later became the Center for Mindfulness) and the director of the prison project with Jon. Over the course of five years and in five different locations, we taught mindfulness to over five thousand inmates, as well as to a host of Department of Corrections administrators and officials.

For me, this was coming full circle. Many of these inmates came from the inner-city pressure cooker I knew so well. These guys were weaned on tension and anxiety. Through the practice of mindfulness, I helped them understand the operation of their minds and emotions, teaching them how to calmly detach from outside provocations and habitual patterns of reaction. Of course I'm not suggesting that people can just meditate their way out of injustice or out of the bad karma they've created. But we *can* cultivate control of ourselves and choose with a clear mind how to respond appropriately and effectively in our lives with calmness and wisdom.

It was during this time working in the prison system that I was approached by Phil Jackson and was brought on board to teach mindfulness to the Chicago Bulls and to other athletes. Now Joseph Campbell's words really rang true: in having the courage to follow my bliss—not knowing *how* I was going to make it but believing deeply in *what* I wanted to achieve—I put myself "on a kind of track that had indeed been there all the while," waiting for me. I stepped back into my original field of bliss: the arena of sports; only this time I came back to it with the consciousness of a mindful athlete and the knowledge that, as Michael Jordan suggested, "that Zen Buddhist stuff" really works. I also came to realize that you couldn't solve problems with the same consciousness that created them. It's only in changing your consciousness that you can solve problems and transform your game, whatever it is and wherever you're playing it.

In many ways, my own path is a reflection of Buddha's Four Noble Truths, which I'll talk more about later. For now, suffice it to say that life brings suffering no matter who we are. But there is a path for all of us that leads out of this suffering and on to that joyful journey of self-discovery, no matter how painful our personal history might be.

THE FIVE SUPERPOWERS

The Five Superpowers are mindfulness, concentration, insight, right effort, and trust. These spiritual superpowers are interconnected and they work together. Buddhism sometimes calls the first three powers—mindfulness, concentration, and insight—the threefold training. Our unconscious mind contains the seeds of all these energies. You can cultivate these three energies throughout the day, in whatever activity you're engaged. Mindfulness, concentration, and insight contain each other. If you're very mindful, then you have concentration and insight in your mindfulness. Generating these energies is the heart of meditation practice. They help you live every moment of life deeply. They bring you joy and happiness and help you to handle your own suffering and the suffering in the people around you.

The fourth power, right effort or diligence, is the energy that makes us steadfast in our practice. Cognitive function improves when we have a positive state of mind. Bringing diligence to our practice of mindfulness is a great way to cultivate positive mind-states. But when we practice sitting or walking meditation in a way that causes our body or mind to suffer, that isn't right effort because our effort isn't based on our understanding.

The last of the Five Powers is trust. It can also be seen as faith or confidence, but the way that I like to look at it is as courage. Having the courage to delve into the unknown and trust what is found there makes the practice of mindfulness and the other powers possible.

As my friend Sharon Salzberg puts it in her book *Lovingkindness*, "Completeness and unity constitute our most fundamental nature as living beings. That is true for all of us. No matter how wonderful or terrible our lives have been, no matter how many traumas and scars we may carry from the past, no matter what we have gone through or what we are suffering now, our intrinsic wholeness is always present, and we can recognize it."[8]

Being a mindful athlete involves living this truth for yourself, because there is no separating who you are on the court, field, or yoga mat from who you are in the world at large. That "intrinsic wholeness" serves you wherever you are and in whatever you're doing. Everything is connected.

MINDFULNESS: EYE OF THE HURRICANE

CHAPTER 2

Let me start with the basics: What exactly is mindfulness? Jon Kabat-Zinn has said quite simply: "Mindfulness means paying attention in a particular way, on purpose, in the present moment, nonjudgmentally, as if your life depended on it." [9] But what's the connection to sports? We all know that the mind can free us or trip us up. If your mind is filled with thoughts or emotions, you step out of flow. Whether you're playing football or a piano concerto, if you start thinking about that fight you had with a friend earlier in the day, or you worry about who's sitting in the audience watching you, you'll probably miss a beat or lose your groove. If someone is talking to you but you're hearing without listening, you'll miss the communication and lose your connection. The minute your mind is elsewhere, the present moment is gone.

But being in the present moment—and being aware or paying attention to what's happening in the present moment—is far easier said than done. Without *paying attention* in a particular way, as Kabat-Zinn suggests, our minds wander, flit around obsessively, latch onto things, and float off. Sometimes it seems like the harder we try to keep the mind in the present moment, the more quickly it slips out of our grasp. Maharaj Charan Singh compared it to a viper when he said, "To control the mind with force is like putting a viper in a basket." But the mind is most often compared to a monkey swinging from branch to branch. We call this "monkey mind."

Monkey mind is actually a Buddhist term that refers to a mind that is restless, agitated, confused, or that is hard to control. It's become a somewhat frequently used term in our high-tech, high-anxiety modern society. Editor Daniel

Smith's bestselling *Monkey Mind: A Memoir of Anxiety* is a recent addition to the proliferation of literature devoted to the perils of the monkey mind. In *Monkey Mind*, Smith writes, "A person in the throes of monkey mind suffers from a consciousness whose constituent parts will not stop bouncing from skull-side to skull-side, which keep flipping and jumping and flinging feces at the walls and swinging from loose neurons like howlers from vines. Buddhist practices are designed explicitly to collar these monkeys of the mind and bring them down to earth—to pacify them."[10]

One could argue about whether or not Buddhist practices are "designed explicitly" to collar and pacify these monkeys, but there's no question that mindfulness helps you pay attention to your thoughts in a nonattached manner, which often takes the emotional charge out of them, slows down your experience of time, and reconnects you to the present moment. It's only in the present moment that you can cultivate conscious flow in your life, achieve optimal levels of performance, and experience that exalted place called "the Zone."

THE ZONE

The Zone has been scrutinized and studied for decades. There's even a Flow Genome Project dedicated to mapping the genome of flow. We're all interested in the secrets of the

Zone experience because it's the ultimate experience of optimal performance in sports. It's also, by the way, a key to eureka moments and breakthroughs in the arts and sciences. And it's a pathway to happiness and a glimpse into something much bigger and far more expansive than ourselves.

Psychologist Mihaly Csikszentmihalyi, a leader in the field of positive psychology and the author of many books, including *Flow: The Psychology of Optimal Experience*, is considered to be the godfather of flow. Csikszentmihalyi describes flow, or being in the Zone, as the act of "being completely involved in an activity for its own sake. The ego falls away. Time flies. Every action, movement, and thought follows inevitably from the previous one, like playing jazz. Your whole being is involved, and you're using your skills to the utmost."[11] He even has a formula for flow that he describes in this way: "Flow occurs when both challenges and skills are high and equal to each other. Good flow activity is one that offers challenges at several levels of complexity."[12]

We can deconstruct the anatomy of flow in any way we want, but the truth of the matter is that it all starts with the mind. Flow is your ability to stay in the present moment. It's a very particular state of mind. The ability to stay present is what fosters the Zone experience. There's no denying that strength and skill are a big factor in achieving high performance in sports, but many players have extraordinary strength and skills. The real key to high performance and tapping into flow is the ability to *direct* and *channel* these strengths and skills fully in the present moment—and that starts in your mind. The flip side of this equation is also true. No matter how strong or skillful you might be, your mind can also impede that talent from being expressed, and it often does so in insidious ways if you don't take care of it. You've probably heard before, and it's true, that the mind is a muscle. You need to take care of it through daily practice. It's that simple and that profound.

SLOW MOTION

If you focus too much on winning or try too hard to be spectacular—which is something most people tend to do—you actually take yourself *away* from doing the things you need to do to get the results you want, and that includes experiencing flow. Former Celtics player Bill Russell has a great description of flow that underscores this point while describing many of the mysteries that make the Zone so compelling.

Russell was a great inspiration to me. We both grew up with basketball dreams in the inner city with poverty and racism as our mascots. Russell went on to become a five-time NBA Most Valuable Player, a twelve-time All-Star, and an Olympic gold medal winner. In his memoir *Second Wind: The Memoirs of an Opinionated Man,* Russell's description of a particular Zone experience is so right-on that I'm giving it to you here in its entirety. "Every so often a Celtics game would heat up so that it became more than a physical or even mental game, and would be magical," he writes. "When it happened, I could feel my play rise to a new level....It would surround not only me and the other team, [but] even the referees....

> *Baseball is 90 percent mental and the other half is physical.*
>
> **—YOGI BERRA**

"At that special level, all sorts of odd things happened: The game would be in the white heat of competition, and yet somehow I wouldn't feel competitive, which is a miracle in itself. I'd be putting out the maximum effort, straining, coughing up parts of my lungs as we ran, and yet I never felt the pain.

The game would move so quickly that every fake, cut, and pass would be surprising, and yet nothing could surprise me. It was almost as if we were playing in slow motion. During those spells, I could almost sense how the next play would develop and where the next shot would be taken. Even before the other team brought the ball inbounds, I could feel it so keenly that I'd want to shout to my teammates, 'It's coming there!'—except that I knew everything would change if I did. My premonitions would be consistently correct, and I always felt then that I not only knew all the Celtics by heart, but also all the opposing players, and that they all knew me. There have been many times in my career when I felt moved or joyful, but these were the moments when I had chills pulsing up and down my spine.... On the five or ten occasions when the game ended at that special level, I literally did not care who had won. If we lost, I'd still be as free and high as a sky hawk."[13]

Everything Russell describes is something athletes experience, in one way or another, at every skill level, and in every single sport. Consider the similarities described by journalist and professional rower Craig Lambert in his book *Mind Over Water.* Lambert writes: "Rowing at its best occurs when you are gliding through the water with such effortlessness and yet such total presence that you almost seem to disappear. Rowers use the term 'swing' to refer to that magical kind of condition when the boat seems to fly over the water and a lot of effort disappears from the stroke. The athlete becomes completely the servant of the oars, the water, and the shell; your individuality—your separate self—isn't there anymore.... Rowing can get you in a state where you're ready to expand your definition of yourself, and I call that an expansion of consciousness. In that sense, you are on the path of spiritual growth."[14]

In the anatomy of the Zone, as both Russell and Lambert described it, here's a breakdown of similar "odd" and "magical" elements:

– They were fully and completely focused on the present moment.

– Time slowed down.

– They could keenly intuit how the next play would unfold without thinking about it, almost like having a "premonition."

– Winning was not on the mind; the focus was on the journey, not the destination.

– Everyone and everything seemed connected in some energetic, unified way: opposing players, referees, boat, oars, water.

– The experience transcended the physical and mental; consciousness expanded and a sense of a separate self went away.

– Performance levels rose.

The more you practice mindfulness, the more readily you set yourself up to experience conscious flow. Put differently, having a mindfulness practice is like watering your garden: it's the only way to make things grow.

THE SPACE BETWEEN STIMULUS AND RESPONSE

Think about the eye of a hurricane, or the calm still center in the middle of a cyclone. No matter how intense the storm or what's swept up in its gale-force winds, that calm, blue center is always there. This is the metaphor I like to use when talking about the space between stimulus and response. We all have this quiet center within us. Mindfulness reconnects us to this center space, where we fully experience the present moment and have access to the transcendent wisdom that's often associated with conscious flow. In his book *Man's Search for Meaning,* neurologist and Holocaust survivor Viktor Frankl famously described it this way: "Between stimulus and response there is a space. In that space is our power to choose our response. In our response lies our growth and our freedom."[15]

Life is all about the stimulus that we experience in the world and the way we interpret that in our minds. We can *react* to this stimulus in various knee-jerk ways—with anger, agitation, anxiety, fear, craving, doubt, guilt—or we can *respond* to this stimulus by getting still, paying attention "on purpose" to what thoughts and feelings come up within ourselves without judgment, and by acting from this center space of calm. The former way of being will keep us stuck in the same place. The latter way of being, as Frankl suggests, will lead us on a path to personal transformation, freedom, and flow.

This calm center space is what anchors the mindful athlete in the present moment and facilitates high performance and flow. Joseph Campbell alluded to it in his conversations with journalist Bill Moyers in *The Power of Myth*. He said, "The athlete who is in championship form has a quiet place in himself. And it's out of that that his action comes. If he's all in the action field, he's not performing properly. There's a center out of which you act; in dance this is true, too. There's a center that has to be known and held. It's quite physically recognized by the person. But unless this center has been found, you're torn apart. Tension comes."[16]

What Campbell means about not "performing properly" when we're "all in the action field" is this: when we have not found that center within, we react to a stimulus from outside with our monkey mind rather than responding to it from that quiet space that we can create between stimulus and response. As a result, "tension comes." We don't perform as well. We get so swept up in what's happening around us, notably all the reactive chatter in our minds, in our emotions, and in our bodies that we lose touch with the present moment and disconnect from that quiet place within. When we lose touch with that center space, we open ourselves up to every possible form of stress and tension. Think about that hurricane again: If you stay in the center, you're fine. The skies are blue. You can think straight, make clear decisions, and respond intelligently and effectively. The minute you step away from that center and into the hurricane itself—well, go ask Dorothy.

We all know that in *The Wizard of Oz*, Dorothy's house is swept away in a tornado and she ends up in Oz, where she has to go on a long, mystical journey to finally get home again ("There's no place like home"). Metaphorically, she has to find herself and her true spiritual center. Her journey back home— or back to that essential center place within—is the mythical journey that we all take in life, whether we're aware of it or not. It's about the quest for meaning, a sense of purpose, love, and connection. Life is about finding our way to this place and living it energetically on and off the courts, no matter what "storms" may happen. Joseph Campbell returned to this idea again and again and in the process inspired a number of artists. George Lucas was a big Campbell fan, as were the writers and directors of the films *The Lion King* and *The Hobbit*.

MEDITATION PRACTICE

Mindfulness meditation involves sitting still, quieting the mind through conscious breathing, and practicing what's called "bare awareness." Bare awareness in the context of mindfulness meditation is the simple act of being aware, of noticing the thoughts in your mind or the sensations in your body in the present moment. For example, when you're sitting quietly, you might be aware that your finger is sore. This is bare awareness. Mindfulness is awareness of the totality of the present moment. For example, if your finger is sore, at first you may focus only on this one piece of your experience: the sensation in the finger. If you practice mindfulness, you may become aware of more going on in that moment as well: Perhaps your heart is working well, your neck is not tense, and there is the sound of wind coming from somewhere. Perhaps that sound makes you think about your home, which provokes a pang of emotion.

We tend to dwell myopically on the problem in front of us. We think that's all there is. When you focus on the totality of the present moment, you become aware that there are positive elements in that moment as well as painful ones. Listening to the wind, you are aware that the wind is as present, as real, as the sensation in the finger, and you can bring your concentration there.

Of course, our minds have a very strong tendency to wander. So you may start with the sensation in the finger, notice the wind, think of home, and then wonder if you left the toaster oven on or think about the broken window at home that you need to fix. Mindfulness requires a returning to the moment we are in, and the breath is the most effective tool for doing this. Mindfulness is a practice, not a destination. Again and again, we bring the mind back to awareness of the breath and stay with the breath, the sensation in the finger, the sound of the wind.

You can practice becoming aware of thoughts and sensations in a non-associative way, with nonattachment, and consistently bringing your mind and attention back to the present moment. It is almost as if you step away from yourself and observe yourself in the moment, and say: *Okay self, I'm experiencing anxiety right now. I can observe this anxiety welling up.* You stay with the experience of the emotion in the present moment by being aware of it rather than reacting to it and getting swept away by it. This simple act is the first step in familiarizing yourself with the practice of returning to and learning to dwell in that space between stimulus and response.

When you practice mindfulness, you become aware that there is a difference between being aware that you are angry or anxious, and being mindful of your anger or your anxiety. To be mindful of your anger or anxiety, you must be aware of yourself "on purpose" and observe your reactions to things in a nonattached way, as if you were observing yourself from outside of yourself. You just notice your own mind and what's passing through it without *identifying* personally with those thoughts and feelings. In *Stillness Speaks*, Eckhart Tolle writes, "Boredom, anger, sadness or fear are not 'yours,' not personal. They are conditions of the mind. They come and go. Nothing that comes and goes is you."[17]

Hip-hop entrepreneur and yoga enthusiast Russell Simmons had his own take on that experience. In his book *Do You!* Simmons describes the observation of the mind and self that comes with mindfulness meditation: "Once you have an appreciation of breathing stillness, and silence, the fruits of meditation will be within your grasp," he writes. "When you spend those fifteen minutes breathing slowly in silence, you'll start to see all your issues and dramas for what they are: distractions.

You might *think* about your job, or your relationships, but you won't get tangled up overanalyzing them. Instead, you'll understand how to let it all go. When your mind is quiet, you can be what the yogis call 'the Watcher.' You're in a state when you can just watch what's happening in your head instead of being controlled by it."[18]

According to Buddhist tradition, this "Watcher" is the consciousness that lives in that center space. It's our capacity to live fully in the present moment and that allows us to "keep calm and carry on." The minute you connect to your Watcher, or your center space, where you're able to make space between stimulus and response, whatever anxiety or distractions you might feel will dissipate. You'll have better control of your responses to things around you—be it a full-on marathon championship or an emotionally charged encounter with someone who pushes all your buttons. Andrew Bynum, the NBA all star who I worked with for many years, calls this "getting my Zen on." Like many other elite athletes, he knows that taking even a few minutes every day to practice meditation in this way will make it easier to *slow down time* and respond better to whatever actions or challenges are happening around you.

Be like water.[19]

—BRUCE LEE

The iconic martial artist Bruce Lee, famously declared: "Be like water." Those three words pretty much sum up the mind-set of the mindful athlete and spiritual warrior who lives life in conscious flow all the time. Water, for starters, responds rather than "reacts." It literally flows. It's powerful, yet it yields to the lay of the land rather than exerting unnecessary force. In fact, it actually gets its force through yielding.

Many people use water and the ocean as a metaphor for our emotional states of mind. Even with the waves crashing on the surface of the ocean, there's always a vast, calm space deep below. When we meditate, we access that inner space within ourselves. Along these lines, Sharon Salzberg wrote in her book *Lovingkindness* that practicing meditation produces a "tremendous change in perspective. At first it is as if we were sitting on the shore and watching the waves dance on the surface of the ocean. Later in meditation, it is as if we are under the water, in the calm, still depths, watching the waves above us moving and playing. Still later we perceive that, in fact, we are the water, not apart or separate, and that waving is happening."[20]

In keeping with the metaphor of the ocean, remember this: Waves only wreak havoc on the surface, or on a very small part of the vast ocean. Most of the ocean is unimaginably spacious, calm, and deep. In the vastness of this space, things that seem gigantic and dangerous on the surface dissipate and even seem inconsequential. There is distance and objectivity—even intelligence, because intelligence is present when you see things from a larger perspective. Mindfulness helps us to "be like water" in this way and to truly understand that whatever waves are rocking our personal boats—or whatever stresses or challenges are flying our way in the practice of our sport—we have a choice to reconnect to that deep place within at all times and to act from that space between stimulus and response. In so doing, we aren't tossed around by those waves. We see them for what they are. There is great power and wisdom in this.

The Olympic swimmer Michael Phelps is a great example of this. He broke his wrist trying to enter a car while training for the 2008 Olympics in Beijing. His coach reminded him that if you can't work with the upper body you can work harder on the lower. So he had to refocus his training to his legs while his wrist healed.

Phelps was diagnosed with Attention-Deficit Hyperactivity Disorder (ADHD) as a child and began swimming at the age of seven partly because his sisters had just joined a swim team and partly to provide him with an outlet for his restless energy. With his wrist broken, he had to choose whether to disperse or rechannel his energy. He rechanneled his energy and went on to win eight gold medals.

Salzberg talks about the accepting and transformative capacity of water even further when she talks about what happens to a teaspoon of salt when it's put into water. When it's poured into a very small glass of water, that teaspoon of salt has a huge impact. But put that same teaspoon in a large body of water, like a lake or an ocean, and the intensity of the impact is dispersed and diminishes because "of the vastness and openness of the vessel receiving it," writes Salzberg. "Even when the salt remains the same, the spaciousness of the vessel receiving it changes everything."

This is another way of suggesting that the more deeply connected we are to the vastness of our own still, quiet center, the less thrown off balance we are by whatever distractions and challenges come our way, big or small.

That said, some distractions and challenges are pretty damn big.

DOING A THICH NHAT HANH: THE INTERCOM BELL OF MINDFULNESS

When I was teaching mindfulness in prisons, I understood what is meant when people refer to a "hell realm." If hell exists, it's here. You could feel the oppression and emotional torment in that place just standing at the gatehouse. Some of the inmates had been locked up 24/7 for many years.

The prison management gave me access to little offices where I could teach groups of inmates how to practice mindfulness meditation. But inevitably during meditation, the Corrections Officer's voice would suddenly come blaring over the intercom, breaking the silence with his authoritative tone. And the second that happened, the inmates instantly reacted and slipped out of the present moment. Whatever that particular Corrections Officer (CO) represented to them—authority, injustice, anger, hatred—the emotional drama and the violence of whatever crimes had landed them in there in the first place all instantly came flooding back. Instead of cultivating peace and serenity in their minds, they were suddenly cultivating hatred or anger without even realizing it. I was sitting there with a group of inmates who'd gone from peaceful to pissed-off in the span of a second.

The program I was teaching in this particular prison used to be voluntary and then it became mandatory. One inmate started every group complaining about having to do something he wasn't interested in doing. I told him he could leave if he didn't want to be in the class and he responded that he would get into trouble if he did so. I reminded him that he could choose to do so anyway and take the punishment (in this case the punishment would have been what they called a "D," a Disciplinary Report). Or, I told him, he could choose to stay for himself, not because the CO told him it was mandatory. This particular inmate ended up being one of those who always came to class early, successfully completed it, and was probably sorry when it was over.

Sometimes life, whether on the inside or outside of prison, is like that CO's voice over the loudspeaker. Stuff comes flying out of nowhere to throw us off our game. So I decided to turn this moment of adversity into a moment of opportunity by doing what I called "a Thich Nhat Hanh." I had the inmates pretend that the intercom was a bell of mindfulness, a reminder to come back to their breathing and the quiet place within. The very fact that it was the CO's voice gave them an even greater opportunity to practice coming back to the present moment. And eventually this is what happened: Every time that intercom went off with the CO's voice resonating throughout the room, the inmates practiced paying attention to the emotions and sensations that arose. They practiced observing them for what they were—*Oh, check that out: I hear that CO's voice: I am feeling intense anger at this moment*—without all the emotional reactivity, or at least trying to step outside of it. They tried to just experience things as they were, without the interference of belief systems.

This lengthened the process of perception, which helped their minds focus on the moment rather than go to that place of emotional overwhelm. Over time it became possible for the inmates to just be fully present with their breathing as the object of their meditation. It was a peaceful and powerful experience for them to be able to sit with the intercom coming on without succumbing to a knee-jerk emotional reaction, and it was surely a practice that would serve them when they got back into civilian life. Of course, there are countless "intercoms" in life that set us off, triggering all kinds of reactions: fear, anxiety, depression, anger. It's easy to blow an emotional gasket or to reach for something to ease the pain. I know because I've been there and done that, big-time. Mindfulness meditation helps us understand the operation of our minds and emotions. It teaches us how to observe ourselves and our habitual patterns in a nonattached fashion, and to let go in order to truly "be like water."

Which brings me back to Bruce Lee, one of my superheroes.

ONE WITH THE TARGET

I was definitely not alone in my reverence for Bruce Lee back when he burst on the scene in the early seventies. I was in college at the time, in that liminal space before I let go of sports and drifted farther away into the hinterland of substance abuse. But I watched that guy Lee on the big screen and, like millions of people, was in awe of his bad-ass Buddhist prowess and spiritual warrior nature. So indulge me here while I take a brief historical flashback to Lee, who had a big impact on our culture and was, perhaps, America's first widely recognized mindful athlete par excellence.

Lee, for those of you too young to remember, was an expert in Jeet Kune Do, a martial art that's predicated on the idea of moving fluidly, like water, and staying perpetually in a Zone state, even in the midst of battle—which is where Lee often found himself, kicking and karate-chopping his way through evil in various movie roles from *The Chinese Connection* to *Enter the Dragon*. Lee was all about the mind-body connection and the idea that the mind is as powerful a "weapon"—if not more so—as the body. He was so intensely cool that he inspired countless Americans to flock to their local dojos for the first time to try to marry mind, body, and soul—and kick some ass at the same time.

Lee is well known for his mix of hardcore athleticism and Buddhist-infused philosophical reflections that pertained as much to sports as they did to life in general. Americans were most familiar with Lee on the big screen, but it was the TV hit series *Kung Fu* in the early seventies that brought much of his thinking to popular mainstream culture. Debuting in 1972, *Kung Fu* was a mystic western that featured David Carradine in the role of Kwai Chang Caine, a monk trained at Shaolin Temple in China, who wandered around the American West repelling bad guys with his spiritual warrior prowess. Despite some controversy in Hollywood, Bruce Lee is widely credited with being the influence for this hugely popular hit TV series.

In one *Kung Fu* scene that dramatized what it means to be a spiritual warrior and an almost transcendentally accomplished mindful athlete, Caine is at a campsite at night with a young cowboy. He's been talking about the connections between archery and meditation, which, of course, the cowboy doesn't quite understand. The scene unfolds like this:

> **Cowboy:** Meditation? What do you think about?

> **Caine:** I think of nothing but to be one with the target.

Caine draws his bow, turns his head away from the target, and shoots his arrow. It hits the bull's-eye.

> **Cowboy:** You think I'm gonna believe that?

Caine: Watch my eyes.

Caine draws the bow again and turns his head away from the target again. This time, he shuts his eyes and shoots. He hits the bull's-eye.

Cowboy: How'd you do that?!

Caine: I do not do it. It is not done.

Cowboy: What do you mean
"It's not done"?

Caine: It is only experienced. It happens.

Cowboy: It happens?

Caine: The pole, the arrow, the bow are
all one. Not many things. Not different
things. One.

Cowboy: Well I see it, but I sure don't
understand it.

Caine: Good.

Cowboy: Why is it good?

Caine: It remains a puzzle. When you cease
to strive to understand, then you will know
without understanding.

Most of us didn't understand what the heck Caine was talking
about, yet we knew that he was on to something big. Caine
became a role model for countless aspiring mindful athletes
who wanted to cultivate the ability to effortlessly be at one
with their sport, like Caine with his bow and arrow. Even a
traditional jock football player could catch a glimpse of great-
ness here. Caine's wise words were Lee's wise words, and
they became a sort of credo for the mindful athlete: "What
you habitually think largely determines what you will ultimately become," Lee said in his book *Letters of the Dragon*,
introducing the idea that our minds drive not only our performance but also our sense of self and the reality we create
for ourselves.[21] He was, basically, playing the "inner game" of
martial arts before anyone had heard of the term.

Lee was inspired in part by a small but groundbreaking
book first published in 1948 called *Zen in the Art of Archery*. It

was written by a German philosopher named Eugen Herrigel and was translated into English in 1955. Herrigel had studied Buddhism and martial arts in Asia before most Americans knew what a karate chop was. His book launched an enduring industry of "The Zen of..." books, including, at the time, the very influential *Zen and the Art of Motorcycle Maintenance.*

In *Zen in the Art of Archery,* Herrigel summed up the mind-body sports connection as it relates to archery in this way: "The archer ceases to be conscious of himself as the one who is engaged in hitting the bull's-eye which confronts him. This state of unconsciousness is realized only when, completely empty and rid of the self, he becomes one with the perfecting of his technical skill, though there is in it something of a quite different order which cannot be attained by any progressive study of the art."[22]

Some American athletes were taking note of this Buddhist concept in Herrigel's book: That it's in having an empty mind and transcending your sense of self that you're actually able to perform at levels way above the norm—while, of course, at the same time you're continuing to perfect your technical skill. One of those people was Tim Gallwey. Two years after *Kung Fu* debuted on TV, Tim Gallwey published *The Inner Game of Tennis,* a hugely successful book that explored the mind-body connection in a traditional sport and officially put the term "inner game" in our vocabulary, while also launching an entire industry of the inner game of nearly every popular pursuit.

In *The Inner Game of Tennis*, Gallwey describes two selves: "Self 1" is the analytical, ego-driven, anxious self that drives many of our actions and preoccupies our minds. This is the self that flits continually out of the present moment, latching onto various inner obstacles and tripping up our game. "Self 2" is the intuitive unconscious mind that transcends these obstacles and allows us to feel at one with everything around us. Self 2 lives entirely in the present moment and holds the key to conscious flow in life. The key to the inner game involves putting Self 2 in the driver's seat and putting Self 1 in the back seat. In so doing, as we play the game of tennis (or any sport) our actions are motivated from that deep, still, and all-knowing center.

So we are back at noticing that center space between stimulus and response, where mindfulness helps us transcend the mental chatter and patterns of self-doubt, and relinquish control to Self 2. This is not easy when you've lived most of your life paying attention to and taking your cues from Self 1. As is the case with any sport or art, the only way to do this is through regular practice. With enough practice, even if you commit to just a few minutes a day, it eventually becomes much easier for you to toggle between Self 1 and Self 2. This is an invaluable technique when you're in the midst of competition, feeling the heat of pressure bearing down, and you want to calm down and access flow even *while* you amp up your performance.

This practice of the inner game can be applied in all areas of life, as Gallwey himself noted. There is no separating who we are when we play sports from who we are in the world at large. When you are flowing and clear in your physical practice, there is a synergetic clarity that flows into other areas of your life. When Gallwey describes the principles of the inner game, he is essentially describing mindfulness: practicing non-judgmental awareness, unlearning bad habits, and learning the art of relaxed concentration.

Gallwey writes, "The player of the inner game comes to value the art of relaxed concentration above all other skills; he discovers a true basis for self-confidence; and he learns that the secret to winning any game lies in not trying too hard. He aims at the kind of spontaneous performance which occurs only when the mind is calm and seems at one with the body, which finds its own surprising ways to surpass its own limits again and again."[23] This intuitive process, says Gallwey, "doesn't have to be learned; we already know it. All that is needed is to *un*learn those habits which interfere with this and then just *let it happen*." [emphasis in original]

I became something of an expert in "unlearning" and "letting it happen." This could only really happen once I'd committed to a regular mindfulness practice. I then learned how to concentrate on breathing life into the present moment, literally and figuratively.

SUPERPOWER PRACTICE ONE: MINDFULNESS

Everything is an inner game. Pure performance starts with the mind. What's in and on your mind determines how well you perform. The center space between stimulus and response is like the eye of a hurricane. The regular practice of mindfulness brings us back to this center space. The more we practice mindfulness, the more readily we can bring ourselves to this center space.

Before you begin to exercise or do your physical activity, take
five minutes to be still and practice being conscious of the
space between stimulus and response. Stop what you are doing and return to your breath. Stay in the calm center. Respond
from the center of the hurricane, rather than reacting from
the chaos of the storm.

CONCENTRATION: FOCUSED AWARENESS

In 2008, ABC cameras caught Kobe Bryant sitting courtside during the fourth quarter of the NBA finals with the Celtics. Sitting just a few feet away were comedians Chris Rock and David Spade. With a super-sized drink in hand, Chris Rock leaned over to Kobe and tried his best to distract him, shooting the breeze and gesticulating in a goofy manner.

But Kobe sat with laser-focus, completely concentrated on the game in front of him. It was almost as if Rock didn't exist—or the roar of the crowd and the chaos around him, for that matter.

Cameras caught a similar glimpse of LeBron James sitting courtside during the 2013 NBA playoffs, only instead of concentrating on something outside of himself, James had his eyes closed and was focusing within, even with the same kind of commotion around him. James was no doubt concentrating on his breathing, clearing a space in his mind so that he could get into conscious flow and sustain it when he returned to the game.

We've all seen professional athletes sitting quietly, concentrating before a game during the national anthem. If they're mindful athletes, most of them are actually bringing their attention, not to the game ahead but, to the present moment: fully concentrating on their breathing and, in so doing, centering themselves in that calm place where they're able to be in touch with the space between stimulus and response. And the reason they're doing this is because awareness of breathing, quite simply, is one of the most fundamental techniques for moving into mindfulness.

Imagine a metronome. Musicians depend on the metronome's regular rhythmic beats to master their scales, which are the basic fundamentals of their music. Now consider your breathing like a metronome, consistently and rhythmically connecting you to your own source and providing you with a regular mechanism for recentering yourself.

Let's even go a step further: Imagine that the space between your inhale and your exhale is that centered place in yourself in which you're able to find space between stimulus and response, the calm eye in the center of the hurricane, that place where your Watcher watches and observes itself, rather than reacts. Imagine, even, that in that space you'll find the line to an anchor connecting you to that spaciousness inside that is able to receive, in its vastness, that "teaspoon of salt." The more deeply you focus exclusively on your breathing, the more profoundly anchored you are to that space. As Thich Nhat Hahn says in *Present Moment, Wonderful Moment,* "Conscious breathing is my anchor."[24]

When you connect to that deep place through conscious breathing, you're far less likely to get thrown off by whatever distraction that teaspoon of salt represents—whether it's Chris Rock trying to get your attention or the static of an emotional challenge. You even start to become aware of things deep within yourself that you might not even have *known* were tripping up your game—certain types of negative self-talk that have been in your head since childhood, established mental patterns, and deep-seated fears.

Through conscious breathing, or what I call Awareness

of Breath (AOB), concentration and relaxation coexist. This helps you take your body where it needs to go and give it up to Self 2. With the regularity of that metronome, as you bring your awareness fully to each breath, you bring your mind back to the present moment; whatever surface distractions may be there dissipate in the vastness of the present moment, and your perception of the things around you starts to slow down. This is not just theoretical; it's actually physiological.

AWARENESS OF BREATH

Breathing is the first thing we do when we're born into this world and the last thing we do when we move on. If we don't breathe, within a few minutes we are no longer alive. It is estimated that we take between seventeen thousand and thirty thousand breaths a day—usually without even being aware of a single one of them.

Meanwhile, every second your breath supplies oxygen to your vital organs, purifies your bloodstream, fortifies your immune system, facilitates digestion, and helps your body release toxins, among many other things. Approached consciously and with awareness, your breath also helps you relax, release stress, and align yourself with your quiet, still center. You can be anywhere, with any kind of stress or chaos, and your breath will always be there like the tides, moving in and out, connecting your mind to your body, and vice versa.

Modern life, with all its stresses, has conspired to shorten our breaths. We have become a generation of shallow breathers. We rush through life and our breathing rushes along with us. Living predominantly indoors, our bodies inhale oxygen-depleted air. Our minds go along for the ride: When we're stressed, our breathing becomes even shallower, which makes us even more prone to stress. It's not a beneficial cycle.

So how does concentration and AOB work with all this? To answer that question, let's stick with physiology a bit longer.

THE BRAKE AND THE ACCELERATOR

Our breathing is controlled by what's called our autonomic nervous system. This system has two parts: the sympathetic nervous system and the parasympathetic nervous system. The sympathetic nervous system is connected to the "fight or flight" response that's hardwired into our DNA and activated by fear, anxiety, and stress. There's certainly plenty of that going on during a competitive game, as well as in the world at large.

When you're stressed or anxious, the sympathetic nervous system goes into action, releasing and literally flooding your body with stress hormones. And when these stress hormones build up, your immune system starts to break down along with your ability to think clearly and respond appropriately. The sympathetic nervous system is the conduit that channels all this stress mojo.

But then there's the parasympathetic nervous system that counterbalances all this. The parasympathetic nervous system basically does the opposite of what the sympathetic nervous system does. Instead of speeding things up and flooding us with stress hormones, it actually slows us down. It lowers our blood pressure and slows down our heart rate. The parasympathetic nervous system actually releases a neurochemical called acetylcholine, which is a key ingredient that supports the process of relaxation.

If you want to conquer the anxiety of life, live in the moment, live in the breath.[25]

—AMIT RAY

Some people look at these two systems like a brake and an accelerator: The sympathetic nervous system is the accelerator, pressing pedal to the metal as we drive through life in fifth gear, fully revved on stress. The parasympathetic nervous system puts on the brakes and slows everything down.

Since our breathing is controlled by the autonomic nervous system, one of the simplest and most powerful ways to activate the parasympathetic nervous system is through our breathing—our conscious, focused breathing. Yogis have known this for millennia. A few of them have even been able to achieve a state of concentration so intense that they can stay in a state of deep meditation without food or water for days. This is probably where we get the cultural stereotype of the guru who sits in seclusion on his isolated mountaintop for weeks on end, seeking enlightenment. The trick for us ordinary folk is to bring that mountaintop experience into our daily lives. Concentration and AOB are the first step in this process.

THE RELAXATION RESPONSE

Neuroscience is finally catching up with what the ancients have known for so long. A Harvard researcher, Herbert Benson, coined the term "the relaxation response." In his book, *Relaxation Revolution*, Benson refers to the autonomic nervous system when he suggests that breathing can even have an impact on our genetic makeup on a cellular level. In the books he says, "It does away with the whole mind-body separation. Here you can use the mind to change the body, and the genes we're changing were the very genes acting in an opposite fashion when people are under stress."[26]

In the yoga tradition, deep conscious breathing is called *pranayama*, which is composed of two Sanskrit words: *prana*, which means life force or vital energy, and *ayama*, which means to let out or extend. On a very basic level, when we're consciously aware of the in-breath and the out-breath—or in other words, the act of inhaling and exhaling—we infuse ourselves with that life force and anchor ourselves in our own deep center space. Our monkey minds slowly stop swinging from vine to vine, because our breath holds sway over our minds. Being in that space makes it easier for us to stay with our conscious breathing. It's a cycle: the in-breath, the out-breath, and the space between the two that lingers. That space is suspended like the pause between two waves, and then the breath comes back like the tide.

At first, the simple act of breathing with concentration can seem impossible. No sooner have you focused on your breathing than your mind slips away and latches on to a thought or sensation, or obsesses over something. Concentrating exclusively on your breathing in the present moment can be a challenge even though you've been breathing every second of your life. If you don't meditate and if you don't believe me, just give it a try: put this book down right now, get still, close your eyes, and focus on your in-breath and out-breath. You'll see what I mean. How long is it before your mind flits, even for a second, away from your breathing?

With diligent regular practice, you eventually become more adept at quieting the mind by consciously and continuously returning to your breathing. Like anything that takes practice, the more you do this, the easier it gets. And the more deeply and consciously you breathe, the more deeply and consciously you activate your parasympathetic nervous system, slowing down your body, infusing it with energy while you simultaneously relax and become more fully present in the moment.

It's as if we enter new territory, or what Buddhist teacher Cynthia Thatcher called "the Country of Now," which is a stand-in for the Zone. In this Country of Now, we're able to keenly focus on what's right in front of us in our practice or our game, almost as if there's nowhere else to go.

Elite players know this experience well. "When you get in the Zone," Kobe Bryant said, "things just slow down. Everything slows down. You have supreme confidence. When that happens, you really do not try to focus on what's going on (around you) because out there (in the crowd), you could lose it in a second. Everything becomes one noise. You're not paying attention to this or that noise. You have to really try to stay in the present, not let anything break that rhythm. You just stay here. You're kind of locked in."

When I first began working with the Bulls in 1993, Bill Wennington had just joined the team. He and I and two other players went out to eat after one of the first practices. We went to Planet Hollywood and people knew the players. Bill is six feet eleven inches and he had on cowboy boots that night, which made him even taller. He's hard to miss. We got our meals for free because we were with the Bulls. I remember someone asking Bill if he was a basketball player because of his height.

Someone asked me if I was Bill's bodyguard. I told them I was his mind-body guard instead. I worked with Bill individually as well as collectively with the whole team. His understanding of the Zone was similar to Kobe's. "You have to be in the moment. You can't worry about what just happened, the basket you missed, the foul you made two minutes ago, because it's over. You can't worry about what's gonna happen the next time down the floor. You have to be right there in the moment. It's most important especially in the playoffs because that's the time of year when you have to live for the moment. It doesn't matter what's gonna happen in Game 3 when you have to play Game 1. You have to be here right now to play basketball when it's happening."

The benefits of being completely in the "Country of Now" are obvious. As Wennington suggests, if you missed a play, it's over. You can't dwell on your frustration unless you want to carry that frustration with you into the next play and trip yourself up with that impediment. Think about it: That past play is gone and the future play has not happened.

In the Country of Now, there are no emotional distractions or anxieties about what did or did not happen. There are no anxieties about what might or might not happen—because the past no longer exists and the future never will (since once the future is there it will be the present). You can only focus on the present moment in the Country of Now. There is no other state. Thatcher wrote about it this way: "To be mindful of the present moment is to stay in the ultimate now, to be acutely aware of what is happening in body and mind at the present instant. At such times you don't remember past events or anticipate the future. Truly speaking, the last breath is in the past. It is gone. The next breath hasn't happened yet. Only the present breath (or sight, sound, movement, etc.) is real."[27]

Concentration on the breath in the context of athletics helps keep you focused on what's in front of you—ball, bat, oar, water, racquet—instead of on peripheral distractions. This is exactly the state of mind you need to start letting go, moving into the Zone, and becoming one with all of these elements. It's a bit of a paradox, because you have to stay focused, even as you widen your peripheral experience in the movement and action of your sport.

One way to look at this, Thatcher suggested, is to consider a juggler: "A juggler's focus is touch-and-go," she wrote. "'Focus and forget it' is the motto.... The juggler has to focus in order to catch the ball. He has to know where to put his attention, and then keep his mind on that spot. While the next ball is coming toward him, he can't think about the last one. He'll fail if he's distracted by a noise or his gaze drifts away. The meditator, too, has to keep his attention in the present moment or he'll drop the ball—that is, become distracted from the meditation object."

I'm reminded again of Kobe Bryant looking almost as still as a totem pole while Chris Rock tried to distract him and take him off his game. He didn't take the bait. He didn't focus on the noise around him or the fastball that Rock was trying to throw. He probably wasn't thinking about a play he made in the previous quarter, either, or what he ate for breakfast that morning. He was not attached to the realm of distraction. Kobe did not drop the ball.

Of course, some of the biggest and most insidious distractions come to us not from the outside, but from the inside—the inside of our own heads, that is. All of our mental chatter and negative self-talk gets in the way of our focus. When we miss a ball and we think, "You're such a loser," or whatever it is we say to ourselves, our focus falters. We step out of the Country of Now.

> *The mind*
> *has to be*
> *empty to*
> *see clearly.*[28]
>
> **—KRISHNAMURTI**

We have to step back into mindful concentration and let go of these distractions each time they pop into our mental sphere. We need to let them go, and not look back and dwell on them, so we can keep moving forward in the present moment. Thatcher's juggler metaphor also describes this ability to let go. "As soon as the juggler catches a ball he lets it go," she wrote. "Otherwise how could he catch the next one? His attention doesn't stick. He keeps it moving, jumping from one object to the next. What kind of performer would pause to gaze at the ball he'd just caught, unwilling to surrender it because he liked the color? Likewise, as soon the meditator notes an object he should drop it, or he won't be able to catch the *next* phenomenon. His attention, although uninterrupted, doesn't cling to anything."

THE PRACTICE

There are different ways to focus on awareness of the breath. The easiest way is to sit comfortably on a cushion with your eyes closed or your gaze soft, and begin to focus on your in-breath and your out-breath. You can also lie down and partici-pate in a guided meditation, walking through an internal body scan, bringing your attention to your breath while breathing into different parts of your body.

I regularly teach AOB to athletes of all types, from elite players to weekend warriors, and often insights come to them with the heightened awareness they're able to generate through conscious breathing. For some of the athletes I've worked with, these obstacles are right on the surface and self-evident. RG, a college golfer, would lose it every time he made a mistake, his performance going from bad to worse because of his own internal negative self-talk.

Through AOB, he learned to relax at will, both on and off the golf course. AK was an Olympic fencer who competed regularly in national and international events in an effort to qualify for the Olympics (which he did). The practice of AOB improved his performance by increasing his awareness of internal self-talk, making it easier for him to observe it, let it go, and get back into flow.

AOB can also help us work through injuries and the emotional fears attached to them. I worked with a collegiate diver who injured her hand on the high diving board. Every time she approached the water after that, she worried about hitting the diving board and reinjuring herself. AOB and other mindfulness techniques helped her concentrate, become aware of these anxieties, and eventually release them and the sway they'd held over her game. Her experience was typical of that of other athletes with injuries that had been caused by continuous overuse or that had simply increased in both number and intensity with age.

This holds true even with more significant injuries that end in physical trauma. Keith Mitchell was a star NFL linebacker when an accident caused a spinal injury that left him paralyzed. He was thirty-one years old and at the top of his game when he experienced the shock of sudden retirement, as well as the trauma of his severe injuries being forced upon him. But while he was in the hospital, Mitchell was introduced to the practices of mindfulness and conscious breathing. "With conscious breathing, I realized that we have to heal ourselves." Mitchell told *LA Yoga Magazine*—and he went on to do just that. Through intense commitment to mindfulness and moving forward incrementally, slowly, and with great determination, Mitchell healed himself "physically, emotionally, and psychologically," he told the magazine. He went on to become a devout practitioner of yoga and meditation.

BLISS STATE

When conscious breathing facilitates flow experiences, we can even get into a bliss state. Music is one of the most universal bliss experiences that we're all familiar with, whether we're actually musicians or not, and it has obvious parallels to the flow experiences that athletes describe when they lose their sense of self and tap into a bigger, more expansive sense of being. In Mihaly Csikszentmihalyi's book *Good Business*, Ralph Shapey, a well-known contemporary composer, described the musical bliss state this way: "You are in an ecstatic state to such a point that you feel as though you don't exist. I've experienced this time and time again. My hand seems devoid of myself, and

I have nothing to do with what is happening. I just sit there watching it in a state of awe and wonderment. And [the music] just flows out of me. It is interesting to note that ecstasy is really the result of our limited ability to concentrate. Our mind cannot cope with too many stimuli simultaneously. If we really focus attention on a given task—whether climbing or writing music— we cannot notice anything outside that narrow stimulus field."[29]

It might seem like a contradiction that "our limited ability to concentrate" should limit our ability to experience bliss or "ecstasy." Many of us equate bliss with not concentrating at all. But pure concentration actually cultivates the bliss state, as paradoxical as that might sound. When we focus on "that narrow stimulus field"—or whatever it is that we are doing in the total fullness of the present moment—we actually summon flow. This underscores the importance of *how* and *what* we focus on.

OUTCOME EXPECTATION

When I tell athletes that focusing too hard on winning can take your focus away from doing the things you need to do to achieve your desired result, I don't mean that you shouldn't know *where* you want to go, or be able to *see* it in your mind. This is what outcome expectation and kinesthetic visualization are all about.

*Phil's got them
Mumphied out there.
You know they wouldn't
be playing that good unless
he had them focused.*

—SCOTTIE PIPPEN

Outcome expectation, for starters, is what it sounds like: focusing on what we expect an outcome will be. To streamline it even further, let's say that an outcome can be either positive or negative. If we believe things will work out, we go into a competition or a practice with a positive attitude and confidence. In other words, we expect a positive outcome. On the other hand, if we expect things to be difficult, our attitude will take our cues from that belief and our actions will follow suit, often creating the outcome we expected.

This is a bit like the difference between people who see the glass as half-full versus those who see it as half-empty. These are two very different ways of looking at the exact same situation. The difference is not with the glass of water; it's with the mindset of the person looking at it. If you fundamentally see that glass as half-full, you are essentially looking at the world that way. And if you see that glass as half-full, that is the vision the world will grant you. You will simply see the possibilities in situations. Basic stuff, right?

Let's take it a step further. Say you play basketball. If you expect things will turn out well, you'll approach each free throw with confidence and be more fluid in adjusting or adapting your throw to achieve your goal. No surprise there. If you expect a negative outcome, your attitude will reflect that as well. But there's another key principle that comes into play here, and that's the ability to visualize, through concentration in the context of outcome expectation, what you want to experience.

The brain doesn't know the difference between what we think and what we experience. So if we imagine or think about something related to the past or the future, on some level we will experience that event—including all the emotions it provokes. To illustrate this principle, I often use this example: I ask the audience to imagine that I'm standing in front of an old-fashioned blackboard. I make my right hand into a claw and make a motion as if I'm making contact with the blackboard and moving my hand in a downward motion to make that screeching, scratching chalkboard sound that grates on our nerves so intensely. I don't actually do it, but invariably people in the audience react as if it really did happen, experiencing all of the physiological, mental, and emotional reactions that go along with it.

There is, of course, no blackboard; there is only our imagination—but that in and of itself is huge. This process is called "kinesthetic imagery" or "kinesthetic visualization," which means experiencing things in our body through the mind and thus "mentally rehearsing" something. In the example above, the audience was mentally rehearsing the experience of hearing that grating blackboard sound. When it comes to sports, we can mentally rehearse whatever goal we have in mind. Using outcome expectation as the frame, we actually rewire our brains to reflect that activity as if we were really doing it. In order to be able to do that, however, we need to have concentration and focus.

One simple technique to help cultivate this process can be done through the following simple exercise. I often ask athletes to lie on the floor in relaxation pose and practice the bare awareness of just being there for a while. Using awareness of the breath, I guide them into a state of relaxation, and then ask them to bring to mind a play that they were able to execute either in practice or during a game. I ask them to notice clearly how they felt when they were able to execute that play at their highest level of performance, reliving that play in their minds in as much sensory detail as possible: how they felt, the rhythm of their bodies, the movement around them.

This process is more powerful than it might seem. When you get very still and focused on the present moment, and you recreate in your mind an experience that you want to recreate outside yourself (or outcome expectation)—you're doing two things: you're mentally rehearsing those things, and you're also learning these things in your body. This is a very different kind of learning from the fitful, fretful focus on winning.

IMPLICIT LEARNING

It is vitally important to recognize that when all of this is going on, implicit learning is also. Implicit learning cannot, by its nature, be declared or named but only half-hinted at. Sometimes called declarative learning, implicit learning happens when we learn something without consciously or explicitly being aware of it. We may not be able to formulate in words exactly what we've learned, but our physical and intuitive bodies have internalized the learning.

Learning how to ride a bike is a good example of this. We are taught certain moves, but the real learning takes place experientially: by starting, stopping, falling, and focusing on the experience in the present moment. It's nearly impossible to stay balanced and learn to ride a bike if you're thinking about other things at the same time. The act of learning how to ride a bike demands total concentration on the actions we're performing in the present moment. Once we learn how to ride a bike, we never forget how to do it—even though we can't explain the process we went through to learn. We have learned how to do it through our adaptive unconscious, without an awareness of how exactly we've learned. This is in contrast to explicit learning, which is the often dreaded and stressful learning that comes through drills and rote memorization.

In a book titled *Strangers to Ourselves: The Adaptive Unconscious,* social psychologist Timothy D. Wilson describes the adaptive unconscious as a sort of central switchboard where the circuits of implicit learning fire up. According to Wilson, "These mental processes that operate our perceptual, language, and motor systems operate largely outside of awareness." Like the Wizard of Oz operating his pulleys and cables behind the magic curtain, the adaptive unconscious operates behind the scenes, but its impact on our mental landscape is profound as it "gathers information, interprets it, and sets goals in motion quickly and efficiently."[30]

When we learn implicitly, the adaptive unconscious is working below, out of sight, without conscious awareness. The key for the mindful athlete is to preprogram the mind-body connection with a regular practice of coming back again and again to the breath so that the body does its thing without the mind getting in the way. Mindfulness and concentration are the corrective here. With mindful intention and attention, we can rewire the brain and create a neural net that automatically carries out these instructions, thus freeing the mind to be present in the moment. This facilitates our ability to have Zone or flow experiences so we can operate and play on an almost transcendent level, completely in control yet totally letting go.

Numerous studies suggest that implicit learning through the adaptive unconscious works better and faster than learning through our conscious awareness. But there's yet another important principle behind all of this, and that has to do with your *intention.*

INTENTION

From my experience working with thousands of professional and amateur athletes, the number one reason elite performers succeed, skill and resources being equal, is their desire and the *intention* to succeed. Intention is what motivates players to do what they have to do, even if it means pushing themselves out of their comfort zones—in fact, *especially* if it pushes them out of their comfort zones.

Intention is purely mental. When you marry intention with positive mind-states through outcome expectation, visualization, and practice, you're able to achieve great things on and off the court. Often these things come incrementally. Remember that taking small steps, consistently, in the right direction will eventually yield big results. That said, you have to have motivation and intention behind these small things. If you do, you're able to achieve success despite the odds against you.

Jared Dudley was a good example of this. Jared used to attend Boston College. He wasn't a top player at first. His brother once told me: "Yeah, when he was a little fat kid in the eighth grade, he told me he was going to play in the ACC (Atlantic Coast Conference) and the NBA." No doubt, people laughed him off.

When Jared graduated from high school, he only received basketball scholarships from midmajor colleges—not the ones he wanted—so he thought he'd end up in prep school. But back in Boston, things were happening that would seal Jared's fate. When a top freshman recruit notified Boston College Head Coach Al Skinner that he was transferring to another college, Boston College coaches turned to Jared.

Jared thrived at Boston College. He expanded his basketball and academic skills each year, and was voted ACC Basketball Player of the Year when he was a senior. He was the first men's basketball player from Boston College to win top player in the league. He later made it to the NBA. Not bad for that fat little eighth grader who ended up getting recruited in mid-August shortly before almost beginning a prep-school career.

The reason Jared thrived despite the odds against him is that he had the intention—even when the odds had been stacked against him in middle school—to achieve his dream. He wasn't even necessarily superathletic compared to other elite athletes. And yet in the end he could guard shooting guards like Kobe. I used to scratch my head watching him and think, "This guy was at Boston College for four years. He was never known as a great defender. Now he's guarding Kobe." But he was smart and he had intention. He thought, "Okay, what do I have to do to make this team? What does my team need?" Then he went out and developed that skill set. He sought out and achieved excellence—but it was intention and a sense of purpose that were fueling his fire.

This was clearly Jared's case. Intention and purpose fueled his actions. He didn't focus or dwell on all the reasons why he couldn't perform or get where he wanted to be. He saw that glass as half-full and related to the universe that way. And the universe responded in kind. Some say this is part of quantum physics: What comes back to us is determined by the thoughts and intentions we put out.

Attention always follows intention, but you also have to *believe* that you can achieve those intentions. You have to be able to see it first. But concentrating and focusing on a clear intention is where to start.

WHAT'S YOUR BODY SAYING?

Some people say that they don't know what their intention or purpose is, but often they simply haven't spent enough time listening to themselves carefully and in silence. Deep Listening is very useful here. Deep Listening is the practice of stopping and listening without judgment or advice. Before you can listen deeply to someone else, you need to begin by deeply listening to yourself. Sit down, clear your mind, and ask yourself in silence: What do I *really* want? What is my life for? Intention will emerge if you go deep enough. Nearly every single elite athlete or successful individual I've worked with had intention and a clear sense of purpose. They knew their charter, their reason for existence.

With Deep Listening, you have an opportunity to honestly evaluate yourself. When you have an experience, take the time to ask yourself, "Am I deluded or is this really happening?" After you have listened to yourself, you may then want to ask someone else. It's my experience that this is why we have good friends, teachers, and teammates. We need to be able to talk to each other, because we have blind spots. So if we have people in our life we trust and who can point these out to us, then we can investigate to see what's true. That's what this practice is about: bringing in the quality of investigation to see what is true and what's going on. If we listen deeply we can observe a habit or an action without being identified with it and without pushing it away or pulling it in. We can just observe and ask ourselves, "Okay, what would happen if this is true?"

As athletes, we really need to take more time than we currently do to listen to our bodies. If you have pain in your body, whether it's tendonitis, a headache, or a cramp, don't struggle to get past it. Stop and listen to your body; surrender to being with what is. Ask yourself, "What is the lesson for me to learn here?" "Have I been overdoing it in practice?" "Have I been going too hard or too long?" Your body is like a circuit breaker; injury is its way of protecting you and telling you to change something. Learn to listen and to trust that still, small voice inside, the voice of self-knowing. You may slow down in the short run but it will keep you far healthier and more active in the long run.

As you learn to listen to yourself and practice, you will find you can listen better to others, whether it's your boss, your child, or your teammate. When you really listen to a person without judging or interrupting, it may feel as though you're hearing them for the first time.

Every high-performing mindful athlete knows that you if want to achieve something, there's a good chance that you can, no matter what, if—and this is a big if—you're willing to pay the price. You not only have to focus on your intention, but you also have to be willing to get up early in the morning and do the same thing thousands and thousands of times—and then another thousand times—*with* intention. Which leads me to deliberate practice.

DELIBERATE PRACTICE

Arnold Schwarzenegger once said that lifting one weight with total consciousness is equal to ten lifts without being totally conscious. And that's because it's not easy to be conscious, and it's not easy to focus on one thing over and over and over again. This is true in other sports as well. When I worked with Kobe Bryant, he was making about thirteen hundred three-pointers a day in the off-season when he was working on his three-point shot. During the season he had hurt his hand so he couldn't even hold the ball. In the middle of the season he changed his shot and still shot a high percentage. Kobe and Michael were very different players. Michael was like a cat and Kobe was like the fast, venomous snake called the black mamba, which became his nickname. But they both had a commitment to excellence and deliberate practice. So what exactly is deliberate practice?

Let's start by breaking down the word "deliberate." It means that something is done *consciously* and *intentionally*. So the first part of deliberate practice involves focusing on and practicing *one specific thing* that you want to improve in your game—and *practicing it with intention and concentration*, mentally visualizing or rehearsing while you practice and thus experiencing the move in your body. Again, the brain doesn't know the difference between thoughts and experience, so in mentally rehearsing an experience, you are sending messages to your body about the specific outcome you want to experience—and in a certain way, you are experiencing that outcome.

But if you want those messages to be ingrained in your body—so ingrained in your body that what you're working on improving becomes almost second nature so that you can therefore let go of your mind because your body knows what to do—you have to practice that thing over and over again deliberately, which means with concentrated focus, steadiness of mind, intention, and a willingness to push yourself out of your comfort zone.

It doesn't matter if you're short or thin, if you were born in a ghetto or with a silver spoon in your mouth—that's not what counts. In a paper titled "The Role of Deliberate Practice in the Acquisition of Expert Performance," psychologist and scientific researcher K. Anders Ericsson explores physical attributes and their possible impact on performance.

I fear not the man who has practiced 10,000 kicks once, but I fear the man who has practiced one kick 10,000 times.[31]

—BRUCE LEE

"We deny that these differences are immutable, that is, due to innate talent," he wrote. "Only a few exceptions, most notably height, are genetically prescribed. Instead, we argue that the differences between expert performers and normal adults reflect a lifelong period of deliberate efforts to improve performance in a specific domain."[32]

Let me restate that. High performance is less about physical attributes and more about what you bring to the table when you commit to deliberate practice.

Ericsson has identified four key elements of deliberate practice: motivation, knowledge, immediate informative feedback of your performance, and repetition. The key take-away here is that physical limitations are not really a primary concern; it's your mindset and internal perception of self that galvanizes your practice and determines how well you perform.

Of course we've all heard by now that it takes around ten thousand hours or ten years of deliberate practice to master anything, whether it's to become an elite athlete, a master painter, or an expert in any field. The NCAA (National College Athletic Association) states that players should practice twenty hours a week. Really? I'm fond of saying to people who want to play at the next level and really excel, that twenty hours a week won't cut it. It's like mastering the piano; to do so, you have to play your scales so well, over and over and over, that they are almost hardwired into your mind-body. If you say: "Well, I'm bored playing those scales," then you've got to examine your commitment, intention, and the concentration behind it. It's only by doing repetitions that we learn.

Learning is circular in this regard. We go over and over the same terrain, each time picking up more intelligence and information, even if we're unaware of it. Remember, this is what implicit learning is all about. You might not think you're making any progress, but your adaptive unconscious is in overdrive, and new patterns of excellence are being laid down and reinforced with every repetitive cycle of practice, no matter how boring it might be.

Every single elite player does this. Back in the day, I recall when Dr J went to play for the Pan American team, which is now called the Olympic Development Team. He told me that they'd train continuously for weeks on end, doing all kinds of drills, practices, and skill-development activities. As good as he was before he left to play on that team, he naturally came back even better.

Malcolm Gladwell, author of *Outliers*, among other books, wrote about National Hockey League players who are born in January, February, or March, early in the year. They excel because they're six or eight months older than boys born in the latter part of the year—kids born earlier in the year are identified as elite only because they are bigger and stronger. They therefore get better coaching, have more opportunities to compete against high-level players, and—the key point—they end up putting in many more hours than players born earlier in the year. One way for the younger players to catch up would be for them to engage in an equivalent number of hours of deliberate practice, with the conscious intention of keeping up.[33]

Mindfulness helps us stay in the present moment, focused on our purpose. When distractions or self-talk get in the way—whether it's "my body hurts, or I'm done doing this" or "I'm bored out of my mind" or any variation on that kind of a theme—mindfulness helps you look at those feelings with nonattachment, release them, and return your focus to the present moment and your deliberate practice: doing your thing consciously and with intention, no matter what comes up in your mind, over and over again. That means breaking down the fundamentals of your sport and your practice into discrete parts and putting in your time with conscious focus. When I teach deliberate practice, I'm not interested in hearing athletes get upset about what they did or did not do. I'm interested in hearing how they investigate what they did and how they will do "error correction" in such a specific way that they can visualize it happening.

ROMANCING THE DISCOMFORT ZONE

We all know what error correction is. Let's say you're a golfer who's always slicing. If you apply deliberate practice to that move, work on error correction consciously and intentionally, the mistakes you make will eventually tell you what you need to work on—and how. The process is like a missile that self-corrects. But we have to know the fundamentals of what we're doing—and then we have to repeat them over and over again, each time moving incrementally out of our comfort zones.

It's helpful to have a coach or somebody who knows how to get you outside of that comfort zone so you are always pushing the envelope and evolving. This is a principle in sports and in life: if you get too comfortable in life, you don't grow. That's the virtue, as I mentioned earlier, of having your ass on fire. For those who have to hit rock bottom to be motivated to change, this is the gift of desperation. You'll do anything to change. You're used to living outside your comfort zone, so in some ways you have a certain built-in resilience.

The thing is, if you're comfortable, and you just want to stay that way, that's fine. But if you want to pursue excellence and high performance, then you have to be willing to get uncomfortable. For some elite athletes it's not even a question of will; they love to get out of their comfort zones and thrive on pressure. That was one of Michael Jordan's defining characteristics: how much joy he could find in being in a challenging, pressure-filled situation.

Love it or not, to learn, you've got to take risks and stretch yourself. You've got to romance the unknown and concentrate on pushing the envelope so that you can attain new skill sets and more readily access flow even under the most trying circumstances.

I've worked with many people individually and in groups who have come to me for help, but who bail out when the going gets too tough. I understand why they leave: because they never get comfortable with being uncomfortable. In fact, many individuals want to change, but they're often unconsciously attached to their suffering or to the old self they think they want to change. They have identified with that suffering or that old self for so long that they're afraid they won't know who they are without it—even if that suffering or that old self has no real place in the context of their current life anymore. That's something of an existential issue, which I'll cover in the following chapter.

History is full of examples of people who, with incredible mental control, were able to step way, way out of their comfort zones because they had to, and who still came out strong. Until recently, Alice Herz-Sommer was the world's oldest pianist and Holocaust survivor. The award-winning documentary *The Lady in Number 6* tells the story of her life. Alice suffered nightmarish indignities during the war—experiences few human beings have suffered or have witnessed—yet her mental disposition, fueled by her intense passion for music, helped her not just to survive, but to thrive. "I have lived

through many wars and have lost everything many times—
including my husband, my mother, and my beloved son," she
said. "Yet, life is beautiful, and I have so much to learn and
enjoy. I have no space nor time for pessimism and hate."[34]

In Jules Evans's book *Philosophy for Life and Other Dangerous
Situations*, similar experiences are described involving people
whose mindsets allowed them to survive unimaginably fright-
ening situations. Evans describes the capture and subsequent
imprisonment of flight surgeon Rhonda Cornum whose heli-
copter was shot down during the First Gulf War, crashing in
the Arabian Desert at 140 miles an hour. According to Cornum,
the only way she survived was by concentrating her mind.
"'When you're a POW, your captors control pretty much everything about your life,' she said. 'I realized the only thing
I had left I could control was how I thought. I had absolute
control over that.'"[35]

Evans goes on to cite diverse people, from ancient Greek
stoic philosophers to Martin Seligman, the founder of Positive
Psychology, whose concept of resilience, as Evans points out,
"is based on the idea, originally from Greek philosophy and
then picked up by CBT (Cognitive Behavioral Therapy), that
you can teach people how their beliefs and interpretive styles
lead to their emotional responses." Many of our beliefs are tied
up in our self-concept. If we believe we can move out of our

comfort zones, then we can, and we do. Not surprisingly, Evans draws parallels to Buddhism, pointing out similarities that include freeing ourselves from attachments, maintaining a "calm benevolence in all circumstances" and living fully and experiencing happiness in the present moment, rather than focusing on the future or obsessing over—and blaming—the past.

Pete Carroll, coach of the Seattle Seahawks football team, has credited the team's resilience and adaptability in part to the team's unique use of mindfulness training. In an article in *Mindful Magazine*, Carroll said, "I'm trying to create a really thriving environment. That means making it as rich as possible. So there's noise, competition, activity, and energy—like when we play. It's better than a pristine vacuum-type environment, as far as I'm concerned. Because we never play there. We don't talk about mindfulness that much, but that's how we operate. We focus on what's right in front of us. We don't care about the other team or the environment we're playing in. We just take every game as if it's the most important in the world and focus right on that. That takes great mindfulness." [36]

GROWING PAINS

Without a sense of urgency behind your intention to push you out of your comfort zone—whether your intention is to survive or just to perform your sport to the maximum level of your potential—you will have trouble sustaining the effort required to tolerate the discomfort of growing pains. That's the case even if something is scary, which might be what Eleanor Roosevelt meant when she said: "Do one thing every day that scares you." If there's no romancing the discomfort zone, there's no growth. That's just how life is. It's like that familar saying: no pain, no gain.

But I'm not suggesting that you have to be in actual pain, or that this kind of change needs to be excruciating. One of the hallmarks of mindfulness is that we can find a middle way; we can consistently push ourselves just enough to achieve those incremental changes, but not so much that we overexert or otherwise injure ourselves.

Overstriving has inherent stresses and pressures that can backfire. Learning to concentrate in stillness and listen to our bodies is the path that leads us to being comfortable with discomfort and being able to stay on the path of making incremental changes. It's also what it takes to turn personal suffering into a joyful journey of self-discovery.

POISE

The convergence of the principles I've outlined—concentration, outcome expectation, visualization, intention, and deliberate practice—are the secret of pure performance. When they are all present, you get the ultimate form of diligent concentration, which I think of as poise. Poise is the ability to keep calm and stay connected to that center space at all times, without getting thrown off-balance. When we *do* get thrown off-balance, we remember to come back to the fullness of the present moment through conscious breathing and mindful meditation.

One of the problems with practicing meditation and cultivating mindfulness and concentration is that you can't see or measure them. People often say, "Oh, this doesn't work, I don't see immediate results," or "This is internal soft woo-woo stuff." But it's like planting seeds. You don't actually see them growing. When they first sprout, they're under the surface, invisible to the naked eye, but you know that with time and the proper attention and care, they will grow and bear fruit. You can imagine quite clearly the tree or plant it will become. The same principle applies when it comes to mindfulness and concentration. Eventually, the regular practice of mindful concentration will reveal what's hidden in our own emotional blueprints, and in so doing, will lead us to even greater levels of self-knowledge, personal growth, and above all, wisdom.

SUPERPOWER PRACTICE TWO: CONCENTRATION

When you quiet the mind and give it one thing to focus on, you quiet your body. When you quiet your body, you quiet your mind. When the mind and body are quiet, there is synergy that feeds pure performance.

Practice concentrating on one of the below items for one minute. Just one minute is plenty to start. If you can do that without your mind wandering, try two minutes, and then three. Perhaps how hard it is will surprise you.

Concentrate on one:

Thought in your mind.

Concrete thing you are doing (walking, sitting, chopping carrots).

Outcome you wish to achieve that day or one intention for that day.

CHAPTER 4

INSIGHT: KNOW THYSELF

I'm constantly amazed at the number of athletes I work with who are exceptionally skilled and highly talented, but who don't play that way because they don't see themselves that way. They don't have a clear sense of purpose or understand that how they see themselves creates their reality. If you tell yourself that you're not good compared to others, or if you attribute your good fortune to luck alone, your self-concept probably needs re-examining. Also it's important to have a clear sense of purpose; just like a lighthouse, it will steer you in the right direction. If you don't have a clear sense of purpose, it doesn't mean that you've been operating without purpose. Instead, it probably means that you've been operating out of unintentional belief systems.

Back in the day, a common thought-form in people's minds was, "I'll believe it when I see it." Now we're finally coming around to embracing the flip side of that idea: "You'll see it when you believe it." Motivational speaker Dr. Wayne W. Dyer might have popularized that expression with his book of the same title (*You'll See It When You Believe It*), but this has been a spiritual principle for some time. Mahatma Gandhi once said, "Your beliefs become your thoughts; your thoughts become your words; your words become your actions; your actions become your habits; your habits become your values; and your values become your destiny." The mystic Edgar Cayce said the same thing this way: "The spirit is the life, mind is builder, and the physical is the result."[37] And Henry Ford bottom-lined it in his own way when he declared that if you believe that you can or can't, you are right.

Belief is a tricky thing. Your beliefs ultimately become your habits—and that includes habitual *thinking*. So if you don't like where you're going, you have to look not just at those habits, but you have to go deeper and investigate the beliefs behind them. Then you have to go *deeper still* and investigate and understand the emotional blueprint on which those beliefs have been built. It's like opening up the engine of your car rather than just looking at what's lighting up on your dashboard.

Because here's the deal: We all have emotional blueprints that have been laid down since childhood, and it's here that we find the patterns and limited thinking that create our inner obstacles that make it difficult for us to believe in ourselves or to readily *see* ourselves clearly. These include deep insecurities, subtle self-critical messages, and negative self-talk that are always there, under the surface, ready to flare up, trip us up, and validate our unworthiness at the slightest mishap.

Sometimes these emotional patterns have been ingrained in us for so long that we're unaware of them, even if they are the cause of our suffering, and even if they have no relation to the person we truly are today. Needless to say, these belief systems not only create and reinforce our own reality, they also determine in large measure how we play the game of life both on and off the court, as well as how easily we can go into flow and experience the Zone—or not.

In fact, as I mentioned in the previous chapter, sometimes we can become so attached to our suffering that we actually *identify* with it. Without our suffering, we don't know who we are, and so we unconsciously cling to it and ultimately create, as Gandhi suggested, the thoughts, habits, and actions that become our destiny.

> *Meditation brings wisdom; lack of meditation leaves ignorance. Know well what leads you forward and what holds you back, and choose the path that leads to wisdom.*
>
> —BUDDHA

It's also in these blueprints that we find the real roots of stress—whether mental, emotional, or physical stress—and not just its symptoms. As I shared with you earlier, I'm an extreme case in point. I had to fall down the rabbit hole and hit rock bottom with my ass on fire before I started paying attention to the real root cause of the pain that I'd become so adept at masking with drugs. Through the practice of mindfulness, I began to see the emotional blueprint of my life in ways that had entirely eluded me before. My self-concept was formed during childhood, when speaking out was a dangerous proposition. As a result, I perceived the universe as fundamentally unsafe. I believed this on some level, and so I unconsciously perpetuated my view of a dangerous universe for myself through my increasing drug use. Fear became part of the operating system of my life, and so I unconsciously manifested it.

Were it not for my commitment to mindfulness, I might not be here today to write about it. Cultivating insight and accruing wisdom about our inner lives is the only way to become aware of the blueprints that have laid the foundation for our enduring beliefs and internal obstacles. In other words, *know thyself!* Mindfulness helps us do this. By creating more space and "spaciousness" in our lives, we're able to eventually get in touch with that Watcher within who observes us. Imperceptibly but inevitably, we become aware of implicit motives and powerful belief systems that operate under the surface, just below our consciousness, shaping our reality for better or for worse.

As an athlete you can always go back to practicing the basic fundamentals of your sport when you're struggling with internal obstacles. This is true in any profession or area of learning and practice; it's always good to go back to the basics. You can also talk about it; I often have elite athletes come together to communicate how they feel about the mental pressures of competition. "It was good because it gave people a chance to talk about things that might be on their minds—the hype, the pressure," Kobe has told me. "I think it's good for them to talk about those things. It increased our performance a lot. It helps us get issues out of the way before they even start." On the pressure of performance that can corrode not just individual but team performance, Kobe added, "Once it creeps into your team and teammates, it can be destructive. Some people know how to handle it, some people don't. The pressure can get to you. When you feel it, it's how you deal with it. You have to prepare yourself as well as you can."

MOVING FROM DESIRE TO ACTION

The wisdom we cultivate when we are able to truly see and understand things about ourselves is fundamentally important for mindful athletes. Because, as I mentioned earlier, there is no separation between who we are as people in the world at large and who we are as players, on the court, in the fields, on water, in snow—whatever our choice of athletic bliss might be.

We have to slow down and pay attention to our behavior, on purpose and without judgment, in order to understand and know ourselves in a more concrete way.

Let me start with a simple example: For many years, I kept saying that I wanted to lose weight, but to no avail. I couldn't turn that desire into action.

Here's what changed all that: I got diagnosed with Type 2 Diabetes. Suddenly, my ass was on fire again and I lost more than thirty pounds. I had to overcome my own habits and behaviors. In order to do this, I had to plug into a new power source. For me, that power source was a burning desire to be free and to be able to do the work I was put on this Earth to do.

Plugging into that power source didn't mean that I instantly changed. I had to look deeply at the things in my own emotional blueprint, including my own particular suffering, that were feeding my weight. So let's take this a step further with a similar example: Let's say you've been overweight your whole life and have always dieted without a long-term result. I'll bet you top dollar that the reason those diets didn't work is because they were just surface remedies. The real problem is wrapped up in emotional suffering, or in whatever emotional hunger you've literally been feeding your whole life. What feelings are you filling up or compensating for through food, that might have been with you since childhood? Maybe you've felt unloved or unsafe or lonely; maybe you've felt insecure and neglected.

Whatever that cause might have been, food grounded

you—literally and figuratively. You unconsciously began to identify with your suffering and with being overweight— and a cycle kicked in. Your emotional suffering became your emotional overeating, which became your habit, which became your weight gain, which became your identity and beliefs (I am unlovable because I'm fat), which became your thoughts (I'm fat because I'm unlovable), which became your destiny, as Gandhi said a few pages ago.

Basically, what I'm suggesting is that we all have our personal form of suffering. Suffering is a part of life and there's no way of avoiding it. If we want to evolve as human beings, we have to understand the wisdom that's hidden in this suffering— and that includes knowing what is feeding this suffering—and commit to a path that leads us out of this suffering.

THE FOUR NOBLE TRUTHS

I base a lot of what I teach about performance and athleticism on the Four Noble Truths, which are the essence of the Buddha's teachings.

The First Noble Truth is that suffering is a part of life and that life is stressful. That said, we can choose how we react to stress: Insight and mindfulness are the ultimate stress reducers. This is good to know, because when we're stressed, whether it's physical or emotional, we can't perform or succeed. The challenge is finding the root cause of our stress.

The Second Noble Truth is that there's a cause for that suffering. Usually these causes are expressed through cravings, attachments, and unwholesome emotional mindsets.

The Third Noble Truth is that there is an end of suffering. Well-being comes through practicing non-greed, non-hatred, and non-delusion. For me, this is all part of self-knowledge, wisdom, and understanding because it's saying that with insight and understanding, we not only get beyond the current manifestation of our suffering or stress; we can actually move way beyond it to a state of wellness, happiness, and joy.

The Fourth Noble Truth is the Noble Eightfold Path. The Eightfold Path is the way that leads from suffering, which is the First Noble Truth, to well-being, which is the Third Noble Truth. The elements of the Noble Path are: Right Understanding (Insight), Right Thinking, Right Speech, Right Action, Right Livelihood, Right Diligence (Right Effort), Right Mindfulness, and Right Concentration. The elements of the path are interconnected and affect each other. As you can see, five elements of the path are the Five Superpowers.

This path out of suffering involves seeing how our emotional blueprints, belief systems, and habitual ways of thinking manifest in the various areas of our lives. In order to release them, we have to see them and understand them before we can realign our thoughts, motivations, and actions. The only way out of suffering, as Robert Frost said, is through it. We don't run away from the bull, we take it by the horns. Because ultimately, we perform at our best when we're not suffering, so we all have a vested interest in committing to a journey of self-discovery, no matter how challenging or uncomfortable it makes us.

EMOTIONAL HINDRANCES: FEEDING THE RIGHT WOLF

Many of you probably know the story called "The Tale of Two Wolves," sometimes attributed to the Native American Cherokee tribe. I have found it helpful and very similar to a Buddhist practice called "watering selected seeds" or "selective watering." The story goes like this.

One day a man spoke to his grandson about a battle going on between two wolves.

One wolf is evil. It represents anger, envy, jealousy, sorrow, regret, greed, arrogance, self-pity, guilt, resentment, inferiority, lies, false pride, superiority, and ego. The other wolf is good. It is joy, peace, love, hope, serenity, humility, kindness, benevolence, empathy, generosity, truth, compassion, and faith.

The grandson thinks a while about the warring wolves and then asks his grandfather, "So which wolf will win?" The grandfather simply replies, "The wolf that wins is the one that you feed."

We human beings sometimes seem almost hard-wired to feed the wrong emotional wolf without realizing it, and as a result those traits grow stronger. "The human mind is programmed to turn to threats, to unfinished business, to failures and unfulfilled desires when it has nothing else more urgent to do, when attention is left free to wander," Mihaly Czikszentmihalyi once wrote. "Without a task to focus our attention, most of us find ourselves getting progressively depressed. In flow there is no room for such rumination."

The Buddha has a name for such ruminations that impede flow; he called them hindrances. In one way or the other, we all feed these hindrances, or our own personal evil wolves. Some of us are experts at it! The Buddha identified five categories of hindrances:

1. Sensual desire. This is a big one. It can include desires and cravings of all sorts. Of course, as a former substance abuser, I deeply understand craving. But let's recognize that cravings are not limited to food, sex, drugs, alcohol, or other addictive substances. Cravings can be attachments to more intangible but no less powerful things, like the ego-gratification of winning at all costs, having the biggest and best toys, social status, or the way our bodies look. They can be cravings for shopping, gambling, or the constant distraction of computer games.

2. Ill will or anger. This hindrance often messes with our game when we compete, throwing us way off-base. Anger and ill will are toxic; they undermine our lives and cloud our thinking both off and on the court and field.

3. Sloth or torpor. This is the dulling of the mind, inattention, spacing out.

4. Restlessness or worry. The modern cocktail of these two hindrances is anxiety, and it insinuates itself into our lives in many different forms.

5. Skepticism and doubt. This hindrance and the hindrance of restlessness or worry are like a Venn diagram, sharing fear as a common element.

Think of each hindrance as one of those wolves. The more we feed it—and the less aware that we're doing so—the bigger it gets and the more freely it roams around, ruling our lives, tripping us up, and creating all sorts of stress. This can become a vicious cycle, because sometimes the way we *release* stress can be the very thing that *creates* it: emotional eating, boozing, spacing out, competing with aggression instead of love of the game.

We all have wolf-hindrances within, and part of our journey of self-discovery involves knowing which wolf-hindrance we're most likely to feed. The more we practice mindfulness, getting quiet, and staying in that calm center space between stimulus and response, the more keenly we're able to observe our wolves with nonattachment. And the more deeply we observe, the better we are at releasing the charge they have on our lives. The challenge is keeping our desire to move forward in life while letting go of our attachment to feeling good. Wanting to feel good is the seductive part—that's what attracts us and pulls us; it's what triggers the grasping and the holding on.

Every human being and every player I've worked with has some hindrance that he or she is struggling with, whether it's fear, anger, insecurity, negative self-talk, or guilt. Elite athletes often have an additional brand of stress that comes with success: the intense pressure of high stakes and a national spotlight on their every step or misstep. We've all seen some of these athletes throw fits of anger or frustration, feeding their wolves—throwing racquets across courts and raging against their opponents, the referees, or the umpires. Some of these moments have gone down in sports history: Three-time world soccer champion Zinedine Zidane, considered the best soccer player in the history of the game, retired in a fog of humiliation when he lost his temper and head-butted his opponent in the chest.

Zidane's aggression made headlines around the world. "My passion, temper, and blood made me react," he later told the media. Zidane was clearly feeding a few wolves. Unless you practice mindfulness, you'll be unaware of how dangerously your wolves are growing inside you, and you may become like a powder keg waiting to pop.

The jury is out on *what* "the yips" is all about, but I'd venture to guess that bottled-up emotions has something to do with it, as well as what sports psychologist Charlie Maher calls "misplaced focus." For those of you unfamiliar with it, the yips is a condition that manifests itself when a player is suddenly and inexplicably incapable of doing a basic move. It's sometimes referred to as the Chuck Knoblauch Syndrome, after a New York Yankees baseball player who suddenly and seemingly out of the blue couldn't make accurate throws to first base. Pittsburgh Pirates pitcher Steve Blass had a similar issue when he suddenly and mysteriously lost his ability to accurately pitch (that led to his early retirement), as did New York Mets catcher Mackey Sasser.

But the yips isn't confined to baseball. It's afflicted athletes in nearly every sport, from basketball to darts (called "dartitis"). In fact, as I write this, Tiger Woods is making headlines for similar reasons: "Tiger has the yips," declared the *Business Insider* about Tiger's mis-hitting chip after chip following a string of injuries. Tiger's former coach Hank Haney chimed in, saying that his short game had fallen apart as a result. "When you have the yips, you have issues," he said on his radio show after the Phoenix Open. "This isn't going away. This isn't just a turn of the switch. It starts with technique and morphs into something else. It just doesn't go away."

Within each of us,
there is a silence
as vast as the universe.
And when we experience
that silence, we remember
who we are.[38]

—GUNILLA NORRIS

It's quite likely that Hank Haney had it backwards: that it *starts* with something else—some mental or emotional stress brewing within—and then manifests or "morphs" into a problem with technique, since these elite athletes have perfected their technique to a tee (no pun intended in Tiger's case). As long as that mental or emotional stress is allowed to brew, or as long as the athlete keeps feeding the wrong wolf until that wolf becomes monumental (even if hidden under the surface), it just doesn't go away. Not living fully in the present moment—instead focusing on winning or whatever ambient pressures exist—adds to this problem of misplaced focus. Adds Maher about athletes struggling with the yips, "If their focus really is misplaced, it's on results. It's on what people are thinking. It gets them away from the fluidity of the process of the game. As a result, it snowballs. They start to judge themselves. They start to tense themselves up. The end result is that the ball is not going where it's supposed to go."

Internal stresses can clearly shift our focus imperceptibly; when we store too much of them inside and bottle them up, eventually something's gonna give. Sometimes what triggers it may not seem like much. But when the pressure mounts inside, all it takes is one simple additional stress to overload our circuits or be that proverbial straw on the camel's back.

What if I were to say that the practice of mindfulness before a game is as foundational as the practice of the rudiments of your sport? What if every player consistently took a few minutes to sit in silence, concentrate on his or her breathing, and get in touch with that calm center and the space between stimulus and response in order to play the game fully in the present moment?

I'm fond of telling players that the best way to score is to forget about scoring. Focusing too much on the end result—or focusing on anything that takes you out of the fullness of the present moment—is misplaced focus. If you don't know yourself well, and the internal stresses pile up, particularly the emotional ones, the accumulated stress will eventually bite you in the ass.

MISTAKES AND FAILURE

In many ways, mindfulness practice is about letting go. I'm not talking about letting go of pleasant experiences. I'm talking about letting go of conditioned responses that don't serve us, even when we love those conditioned responses dearly. That's why people overdrink, overeat, and engage in sexual misconduct. Often just the thought of the seduction itself is enough to keep us going; we run on the juice of being in that conditioned mode of wanting. We get attached, or we long for things to be a certain way. But the reality is that sometimes we have to sit and watch to see how we get stuck and understand how our conditioning gets triggered, so that we can make a more informed choice the next time we start to get drawn in.

In the realm of athletic performance, our attachment comes up even before we compete. We have to ask ourselves: "What is the feeling I'm craving?" The deeper motivation is the one that will be there independent of the passing emotion. And sometimes it's tricky, because as I mentioned earlier, we can get so attached to our hindrances and our suffering that we identify with them and don't want to give them up, even if they clearly don't serve us. I often work with people who fight vehemently to keep what's causing their suffering. "What do you mean?" they ask. "I don't want to give *that* up."

When you identify too much with your suffering, it becomes you. This is something no one likes to face. But that isn't really who you are. The emotional component, your feelings and sensations, is not the essence of who you are. They are fleeting distractions; this can be said of anger, resentment, or whatever hindrance or wolf is roaming around in our emotional backyard. They are part of the suffering we have habituated ourselves to, but that suffering is not who we are. The same is true when it comes to mistakes and failures.

KNOW YOUR STRESS

Knowing yourself also involves knowing the wisdom of your own body and how you relate to stress. All of our hindrances and inner wolves create internal stress, and internal stress builds up in our bodies. There are reams of data supporting the mind-body connection. Neuroscientists have identified five categories of brain waves that are positively influenced by meditation in verifiable ways that not only cultivate peace, but that reduce stress and the illnesses associated with it that have the potential to undermine just about every organ in our body. "This new science is forcing the medical community to take more seriously the popular notions of the mind-body connection," says Esther M. Sternberg, M.D., director of the Integrative Neural Immune Program at the National Institute of Mental Health in an article for NIMH. "The problem is when the stress response goes on for too long," she writes. "That's when you get sick. Hormones weaken the immune system's ability to fight disease."[39] No doubt that disease can be physical and/or emotional.

I'm living proof that mindfulness is effective in treating chronic, stress-related pain. Of course, you shouldn't get to the point where chronic stress has insinuated itself into your life and undermined your game. But stress comes in many forms and is a tricky beast. There's the stress of competition and training that we all know well, but there are also all sorts of subtle stresses in our personal and professional lives. It *all* has an impact on our performance because all these things are connected.

KNOW YOUR BODY

There is no difference between who we are on the court and off the court. Stress builds up in our bodies no matter what's going on and will express itself in every arena. That's why the wisdom of knowing oneself includes knowing the body. You need to practice your sport or activity and you need a meditation practice, so that you work on your body and your mind simultaneously, building synergy between the two. That way you can listen—really listen—to the wisdom of your body.

Despite everything you've just read, not all stress is bad. Some stress motivates us and pushes us out of our comfort zones in just the right incremental fashion. When this happens, our bodies and minds are pushed in expansive ways that serve our game. Our bodies adapt and implicitly learn. "Adaptability is probably the most distinctive characteristic of life," wrote Hans Selye in *The Stress of Life*. Selye calls this capacity to adapt one of the "great forces" that animates us and motivates us as human beings to evolve.[40]

Selye defines stress as a state within the body that produces observable symptoms, not just vague or general nervous tension. He also emphasizes what should be common knowledge by now: that each of us responds to stress with a particular sign. These signs run the gamut from irritability, inability to concentrate, emotional instability, dizziness, and nervous ticks, to insomnia, stuttering, clenching of the teeth, neck and lower back pain, being accident-prone, nightmares, loss of or excessive appetite, and free-floating anxiety.

Clearly, you have to know your own signs and listen when your body says: *Hey, pay attention, I'm trying to tell you something important.* If your mind is constantly filled with the noise of mental chatter or if you never get still enough to listen to your body, you've got a long row to hoe.

When things get tough and our bodies start to react, we need mindfulness to reset our internal north star. We need to be quiet, listen, and practice conscious breathing to bring ourselves back to the present moment and activate the parasympathetic nervous system, putting the brake on and slowing things down in our bodies. This coming full circle helps us listen to what our bodies are trying to tell us.

POSITIVE STRESS

There's an important distinction to be made between stress, distress, and what Selye calls "eustress." Stress and distress are correlated. When stress is persistent, unresolved, and cumulative to the point of being chronic—whether that stress is physical or emotional—it becomes distress. Prolonged emotional distress can eventually lead to anxiety, withdrawal, or depression.

Eustress, on the other hand, enhances physical and mental functions through such things as strength training and challenging work. This is the "good" kind of stress. Eustress can be described as that space between where we are and where we want to go—or that place between our comfort zones and the fringe of our discomfort zones.

When you physically push your body beyond its present limits, it responds to the increased demands made upon it in familiar ways; you experience shortness of breath, your heart races, you sweat, get tired, maybe feel a few aches. If you continue to push your body in an incremental fashion—ideally practicing intention, visualization, and deliberate practice at the same time—your body will eventually adjust to the new physiological level required of it, thereby increasing your physical capacity. In this way, we set down new neural pathways while increasing our physical skills.

The same is true of our ability to push ourselves mentally. Mentally we can train ourselves to be comfortable with being uncomfortable, to feel calm in the midst of chaos and stay in the eye of the proverbial hurricane. Through mindfulness, we cultivate the ability to more readily access and stay in that space between stimulus and response, rather than react in a knee-jerk fashion to stress. We learn to have a greater tolerance for cognitive dissonance on an emotional level; even in the midst of anxiety, we can experience the feeling that everything is going to work out fine; we might even experience the kind of fear that gives us the courage to walk straight ahead, no matter what. We can even learn to delay or let go of our desire for instant gratification by tolerating discomfort for an extended period of time, even if it's in small increments of less than a minute, much like swimmers who increase their amount of time under water by seconds until they reach that critical minute.

COMFORT AND DISCOMFORT

Our bodies like to be in homeostasis. We like to be balanced. Life is hard enough—we want to be comfortable! But, again, to get better and improve our game on and off the court, we need to move out of our comfort zones. That doesn't mean you should go so far out of your zone that you can't function well. Our bodies work best when we push them in small increments. If we push ourselves too far, eustress can become distress. We have to really pay attention, because they can manifest the same symptoms. Eustress is achieved through moderation, sticking to the middle way, and not going to extremes.

But when we're pushing ourselves incrementally, reaching peak performance takes time. You can't push yourself so far out of your comfort zone that your body breaks down or that you ultimately give up because you can't sustain your own self-imposed pressure. If you crave those kinds of extreme experiences, you might want to question which wolf you tend to feed.

Moving out of your comfort zone through experiencing eustress is a continuous incremental process of romancing your discomfort zone. It's not like you get to a certain level and then stay there. Things are always either going forward or backward; they're not staying static. If you are comfortable where you are and you just want to stay comfortable, that's fine, but that isn't the way to pursue excellence and wisdom.

You can't pursue wisdom without being willing to get uncomfortable. You have to ask yourself with regularity, "Can I do better than I'm doing now? Can I play at a level above where I am now and what I'm doing now?" But you need to ask these questions without judgment. This is not about focusing on what you can't attain. Rather, it's about identifying where you want to be, focusing on that, and pushing yourself incrementally in that direction.

Sometimes I recall that time I left the financial analysis company where I'd worked for years. Everyone else wanted to leave the job, too—they were miserable, in fact—but they'd actually grown too comfortable with their own unhappiness and the mediocrity of their lives or they were primarily concerned with making a living. Their asses weren't on fire. They were too fearful of the discomfort involved in leaping into the unknown and taking risks. That's understandable; sometimes taking a leap of faith feels like you're leaping into the fire. But sometimes you've got to take the leap of faith and jump. As John Burroughs once said, "Leap, and the net will appear."

The alternative, sticking with your unhappy comfort, could be your spiritual demise.

I've heard it said that if you put a frog in a pan of cold water and slowly turn up the heat, the frog will simply keep adapting its comfort zone to the heat, even when the water gets to the boiling point. Eventually, it will just end up as one dead frog. But put a frog in a pot of really hot water, and it will immediately leap out, even if it doesn't know where it will land. Wherever it lands will likely be a better place than a boiling pot of water.

Of course, I'm not saying that we're all operating under such extreme conditions, but the reality is that if you want to change and achieve peak performance, you have to take some risks and push your personal envelope. I've worked with numerous people, both individually and in groups, who've come for help. But as George Gurdjieff, the midcentury influential spiritual teacher, warned, "If a person gives way to all their desires, or panders to them, there will be no inner struggle in them, no friction, no fire. But if for the sake of attaining liberation, they struggle with their habits that hinder them, they'll create a fire, which will gradually transform their inner world into a single whole."

I couldn't have said that better myself. Without a sense of urgency, it's hard to sustain the effort it takes to tolerate the unpleasantness of growing pains. I often remind people that we spend a lot of our time vacillating between boredom and anxiety. If you're anxious, then it probably means you need to get busy developing new skills. If you're bored, you've got to challenge yourself more and push yourself out of your comfort zone. We need to be wary of being on a plateau and not moving on to the next vista because we're daunted by the path it takes to get there, or because we're simply comforted by having reached a plateau.

Again, pressure can be good and some people thrive on it. But in order to truly thrive, you have to know your mind and body. To pursue excellence and wisdom, you've got to continually move out of your comfort zone and persistently push the envelope with intention; you have to visualize the goal that matches this intention while you do this; and you have to establish your intention and believe it, see it, and then move forward incrementally to manifest the goal, setting your own standards rather than following the herd.

Former NBA champion Wilt Chamberlain is an example in this regard; he was way ahead of his time. In 1962, he scored 100 points in one game in Hershey, Pennsylvania. At that time basketball didn't have the three-point zone because no one was making those shots. But he was so dominant, they had to change a number of rules. He was so much better than everyone around him—and he just played and played and played. Twenty years later, when Kareem Abdul Jabbar broke his scoring record, Wilt was asked, "What do you think about him breaking your scoring record?" Wilt's response was, "If I had known anybody had a chance of breaking that record, I would have put it way out of sight."

In other words, he would have focused not on someone else breaking his record, but on his *own* goal of outdoing himself as he continued to push the envelope in his own performance.

In his era, there was nobody to challenge him outside of Bill Russell, and even Russell couldn't challenge him in the way that Wilt needed to be challenged. Even though he was an elite performer, according to his own words he could have taken that standard and made it much higher. It's a problem when we base our standard on our surroundings, on the people who are around us. Comparing ourselves to others can be a good way, at first, to get us motivated. But it's not really challenging us to push ourselves according to our *own* standards, based on our own volition. As long as you're comparing yourself to others, you're not truly challenging your limits.

MAKE YOUR COMFORT ZONE THE HORIZON

I've had the good fortune of seeing many high-performance athletes practice when they were very young, from Dr. J to Michael and Kobe. While many aspects of their game changed over time, they all saw themselves as capable of continuous high achievement. Their comfort zones were like a horizon, always moving forward in front of them as they approached them. And they all had another commonality, serious injuries notwithstanding, and that is the gift of self-efficacy, or the ability to know their limits and develop expertise even when they made mistakes, got injured, or had setbacks. Because sometimes, those hard knocks were blessings in disguise; they were an opportunity to think and learn. It's been my experience with all the athletes I've worked with, from the Lakers and the Bulls, to girls' soccer teams, to weekend warriors, that while there are always calamities, extreme circumstances can make you stronger. This is what's called having a strong sense of self-efficacy: the ability to tell yourself that no matter what happens, you will take everything as a challenge, not a curse. You'll rise to the occasion and say, "Okay, the going is tough but this is going to be great!"

Self-efficacy is tied to the ability to believe and see yourself as capable. It's a core mental strength. Self-efficacy is cultivated when we know ourselves well enough to work through whatever internal obstacles we have, whether that's a negative self-image, an ingrained sense of defeat, or other issues.

Self-efficacy, or stress hardiness, is the galvanizing force behind what I call the three Cs: *Commitment* to your growth and development; *Control* over how you respond to stressors;

and viewing every crisis or pressure as a *Challenge*. These three Cs are mental and emotional pillars of wisdom that help us increase our performance, effectively field whatever fastball might come hurtling our way, and stay in flow.

> *If you change the way you look at things, the things you look at change.*[41]
>
> —WAYNE DYER

When you combine the three Cs with self-efficacy, you not only see crises as opportunities for growth, you also naturally create challenging goals for yourself that support that growth. This keeps you in a high state of awareness, which means that you naturally push yourself incrementally out of your comfort zone. This is what eustress is all about. It's also part of how we learn to look at "failure" and mistakes or crises as opportunities.

EMBRACING FAILURE: YOU ARE NOT YOUR MISTAKES

Failure is what you make of it. Failure can be an opportunity. Mistakes are feedback for learning. If you grow up feeding the wolf of self-defeat or self-loathing, although this may be a hurdle for you, it's an important part of your personal struggle.

Several books have been written that reframe failure in this way. Recently, talk show host and political commentator Tavis Smiley wrote *Fail Up: 20 Lessons on Building Success from Failure*. Like me, Smiley grew up in a brood (thirteen people in a trailer home) and experienced his share of hard-core racial injustice. But Smiley persevered in life and figured out that failure is his friend, and learned to view his misdeeds, missteps, and setbacks as his wisest teachers and most potent growth opportunities. "I have a deep and abiding faith," he told NPR. "But there are some things you can only learn via experience."[42]

One of the many people Smiley quotes in his book about his journey to "fail up" is Michael Jordan on his "failure" commercial for Nike: "I've missed more than 9,000 shots in my career," Jordan says. "I've lost almost 300 games. Twenty-six times, I've been trusted to take the game's winning shot and missed. I've failed over and over again in my life. That is why I succeed." Soichiro Honda, CEO and founder of Honda Motors, looks at it this way too. He once said, "Success is 99% failure."[43]

It's important to remember that although we all make mistakes, *we are not* the mistakes. Identifying with failure is a dead-end. I work on this with the athletes all the time. Some of them instinctively learn from their mistakes and have an intelligence about them that nourishes and cultivates a positive mind-state. When there's chaos, they stay in the eye of the hurricane.

But other people relate to mistakes and failure as if they were a reflection of themselves. They identify with the mistake, internalize it, see it as a validation of whatever negative self-talk or belief systems have been part of their emotional blueprint. With every mistake or failure, they continue to stoke the fire of that particular hindrance; they keep feeding that wolf. When we're in a negative mindset, we see ourselves as failures. Our perspective gets so narrow that there's no way to move forward or evolve, no way to learn from the mistake that will facilitate growth. When this negative mindset—or what can be called an unwholesome mind-state—becomes par for the course, every molehill looks like a mountain; every little thing is a matter of life or death; every imperfection is a problem.

Here's the reframing that has to happen for all of us: We need to recognize failures as opportunities and mistakes as feedback for learning. We need to realize that, like moving out of our comfort zones, failures are potent *Challenges* for personal growth, as well as opportunities to *Control* how you respond to challenges and how you keep your *Commitment* to growth, no matter what. And, by the way, when you move out of your comfort zone, you're bound to "fail"—but with the right mindset, you are always "failing up."

"Imperfection also makes growth possible," wrote Kristin Neff in *Self-Compassion*. "Like it or not, the main way we learn is by falling flat on our face, just as we did when we first learned to walk. Our parents may tell us a million times not to touch that hot stove, but it's only after we actually burn ourselves that we really understand why it's not such a great idea. The learning opportunities provided by failure can actually help us to achieve our dreams. In the words of restaurateur Wolfgang Puck, 'I learned more from one restaurant that didn't work than from all the ones that were successes.'" [44]

Neff regards failure as "life's apprenticeship," a way of discovering something new and reframing crises as opportunities. Psychology professor Robert Emmons takes that a step further, suggesting that even crises or failures that are tragedies can have spiritual import in truly hard times. "The religious traditions encourage us to do more than react with passivity and resignation to loss and crisis," he writes. "They advise us to change our perspective so that our suffering is transformed into an opportunity for growth. Not only does the experience of tragedy give us an exceptional opportunity for growth, but some sort of suffering is also necessary for a person to achieve maximal psychological growth." [45]

Let me repeat that: "Some sort of suffering is necessary for a person to achieve maximal psychological growth." We're back to the foundation of the Buddha's Four Noble Truths.

In a *Psychology Today* article, psychologist Mel Schwartz takes this a step further, pointing out that crises can even pop open the lid we've imposed on our own sense of self. "The crisis literally removes the boundaries that have circumscribed us," Schwartz writes. "It is as if a tornado has swept in, and when we open our eyes, everything has changed. The maelstrom places us well beyond the bounds of the known. We typically find ourselves wanting desperately to get back inside the comfort of the known. But the crisis precludes that option. There is no going back. But that is where opportunity lies." [46]

ERROR CORRECTION

Schwartz goes on to describe crisis and opportunity as "merely differing aspects" of a continuum or a process. Crisis as opportunity is an ancient Asian philosophical principle that many of us may have heard about in one way or another. On a more basic level—in life, in sports—the ability to turn a crisis into an opportunity is the same ability as turning a mistake into a chance to learn.

One simple way to do this is through emotional error correction. In this context, errors or mistakes are stepping stones for growth. The first step in this process involves self-reflection instead of self-blame. Instead of saying to yourself, "Oh crap, why did I just fumble that game? I'm such a loser!" or instead of blaming someone else ("It's so-and-so's fault!"), you reflect and ask yourself: "Well, why did that happen? What can I do to change that?" The former mindset is self-defeating and invites powerlessness, passivity, anger, and frustration; the latter mindset opens the door to exploration and learning, which ultimately brings more energy to your game.

Mindfulness helps us step back, observe those self-defeating thoughts without judgment, and abandon them. But when we are not in the present moment and we're listening to that self-critic, here's what can happen: We can get so keyed up ("No, I've got to shoot *real* quick, because I want to make it") that our energy is channeled through a narrow, tense spectrum. We rarely get into flow that way. On the contrary, we get in our own way. Sometimes you can actually see this happen: I once saw a player trying to shoot before he caught the ball; he was moving so fast that when he finally was able to reach for the ball, he hit it and of course it flew out of bounds. Well, why does that happen? It's because he wasn't in the present moment; he wasn't in the flow.

In situations like this when you're so sped up in your head that you fumble your own play, you have to stop. You have to reconnect to the present moment, just catch the ball, then gather yourself and shoot. That is error correction—even if you miss. You have to focus on what you do in the present moment, not on what you did that's already happened. If you miss a free throw, you shouldn't be thinking, "Oh I missed that! I'm a lousy free-throw shooter." Rather, focus on what you need to change, because that moment of missing the free throw is already gone. It's in the past. Instead of dragging the emotional charge of missing a shot into the next moment, use corrective "directed thought" and change your inner dialogue to: "Okay, so if I keep my elbow in, and change my stance, I'll get into a better rhythm."

It takes courage to silence the self-critic. That inner critic always seems ready to jump in and say, "You messed up. You're not worthy of love or respect," or "You're nobody," or "You're not adequate." That idea or belief system can in itself be enough to prevent you from seeing things clearly and moving from motivation to action.

I've seen hundreds of student athletes who weren't really talented, but because they thought they were—they truly *believed* they were and saw themselves that way in their minds—

they played well. Conversely, I've seen plenty of others who had talent that was out of this world, but they didn't believe it. As a result they would withdraw, close down, and never fully express that talent simply because their self-critic had a vice-grip on their minds.

Remember what Bruce Lee said: "As you think, so shall you become." [47] Seven words of wisdom to keep in your back pocket.

A STATE OF WONDER

High performers often look at mistakes and "failure" through the prism of error correction and attaining more skills, more knowledge, and more experience. No matter how many times they fail, they maintain a mental state of wonder. They keep asking; "How about if I just go and do this and let it speak to me, instead of assuming I know in advance what it is." When we can operate on the principle that we don't know anything but we have everything to learn, we're infused with a sense of wonder. It's like a little kid who's learning to walk: he or she keeps falling down, but then something incredible starts to happen and eventually the child is able to move slowly forward on wobbly feet. Then that incredible thing that seemed so difficult becomes second nature.

DRINKING MY TEA

My tai chi teacher used to ask us to do full splits and all sorts of other difficult positions that, when they were first introduced to me, I was sure were impossible. But she never relented. She used to say to me, "George, can you afford it?" That was her way of asking, "Can you do it? Are you willing to make the commitment?" That's the thing: by making the commitment and moving forward incrementally, I started getting down further and further in my splits, closer to the floor than I'd ever thought possible.

This principle plays out even on the most mundane levels, when simple daily rituals oblige us to stop and reframe things. For example, I drink a Chinese tea that comes in little sealed packets. Sometimes I can tear them open with my hands and sometimes I can't. It's puzzling. This has been going on for a couple of years now. Part of me gets frustrated when I can't open them. "Come on now!" I think to myself. I sometimes have to use scissors and cut them open, or bite their corners. I find myself saying, "How strong do you have to be—you can't rip that?" I would get stuck in that mind-state.

Then one day I thought to myself: Okay, what would happen if I brought the same quality of interest, wonder, and investigation that I do with other things to this teabag dilemma to see what's going on? What if I just say to myself, "Well, how can I do this?" So I started paying mindful attention, and it took me a while—several attempts over a period of time, in fact—but eventually I realized that I needed to hold my thumb differently so that I had a good grip on the packet. Once I did that, the packet easily tore open. It felt satisfying, like I was solving the riddle of the tea packet. I was confronted with a small problem that actually presented me with an opportunity to learn something about myself, and about the way things are. This was also a form of right effort.

We can all transform frustration into the joy and the satisfaction of discovering how things work by converting small daily activities and tasks into teachable moments. We can learn for the joy of learning. If we can do this with a tea packet, imagine what we could do with other things if we bring that same quality of interest, curiosity, and inquiry to the forefront, always asking with an open heart, "Well, what's this?"

NOTICING WHAT'S RIGHT

In the process of reframing failure and practicing error correction, we also have to start noticing what's right. This is another version of the "glass half-full" way of seeing things. When I work with clients, especially with teens, I say to them, "Why don't you catch yourself or one of your teammates doing something right?" Their focus is often on what's wrong or what needs to change, instead of just realizing the beauty in the moment that's right in front of them, with all of its imperfections. Often, however, we don't have time to enjoy that beauty because we're stuck on paying attention to what's wrong.

People invariably ask me questions about basketball offense and making shots. They rarely ask me about defense. When you ask somebody how they played, you don't ask them, "Well, how many shots have you blocked?" or similar questions. You ask, "How many points, how many rebounds, and how many assists did you have?" That's our cultural agreement; we only focus on the offense. We only focus on what's wrong. We only focus on why we *didn't* do something instead of focusing on what we did do or what we learned.

Once we've been able to pay attention to that inner critic without judgment, to see where it lives in our emotional blueprint, why it's there, and how and why we feed our wolves or hindrances, then we start to accrue essential wisdom. We're suddenly able to observe unwholesome thought patterns, belief systems, and attachments associated with our hindrances. And when we're able to bring these things into focus through the practice of mindfulness, we're not only able to abandon them; we are squarely on the road to another key Spiritual Superpower that leads to pure performance.

SUPERPOWER PRACTICE THREE: INSIGHT

Get quiet and get in touch with your emotional blueprint. Get quiet and get in touch with your hindrances. Practice abandoning these thoughts and belief systems. Be wary of getting too comfortable with comfort. Likewise, be wary of getting too comfortable with discomfort.

Ask yourself at least one challenging question each day.
Some examples:

What makes you uncomfortable in your physical activity?
Why? Where do your discomforts come from? How do they
 hold you back or move you forward?

What hindrance do you cultivate?

What do you crave? Worry about?

What emotion is most and least comfortable for you:
Anger? Fear? Guilt? Anxiety?

Where does your stress live? Why is this particular stress
inhabiting your body?

Take some time and listen to your body when you ask these
questions. Don't just answer with your mind. If you listen to
your body, it will answer you.

RIGHT EFFORT: FORGET THYSELF

CHAPTER 5

On the surface, right effort is what it sounds like: exerting effort that takes you in the "right" direction, versus effort that takes you in the "wrong" direction. Think of Sisyphus, that king in Greek mythology who, because of his deceptive and unethical behavior, was condemned for eternity to push a large boulder up a hill, only for it to roll back down so he would have to start over again. It didn't matter how hard Sisyphus clenched his teeth and exerted force, pushing hard against gravity; his efforts would remain the same: frustrating and futile in perpetuity.

The myth of Sisyphus has been interpreted in many ways, but for our purpose let's just say that Sisyphus is exerting "wrong effort." He represents that part of our nature that's conditioned to believe that life is a grind and that to "win," we have to fight our way to the top, focus on the destination and not the journey, and swim hard upstream against the current even if that current loops us back through the same unending cycle of stress.

Sisyphus lives in the land of extremes. In mainstream sports, this is essentially the familiar archetype of the forceful gladiator who must crush the opponent and win at all costs in an us-against-them world of high-stakes combat. Anger and/or fear are what motivate action. There is either victory or failure, triumph or defeat.

For some time I practiced this way—with wrong effort, force, and exertion. I had the "lone warrior" mentality. I sat through pain, I wanted liberation yesterday, I wore myself out both mentally and physically by trying too hard, and then I would be too exhausted to continue. I got really good at looking at whatever was wrong. I had been trained to work long and hard for what I wanted, so being hard on myself and working through pain and suffering was normal. My sense of self was wrapped up in seeing the world this way. And so I continued to see it that way, and continued to create that world for myself.

Contrast this to the idea of the spiritual warrior, epitomized by Bruce Lee and other martial artists who've mastered the art of fighting without fighting. These mindful athletes use their intuition in the present moment to cultivate a connection to the Zone, always focused on the journey, not the destination. In consciously going with the flow (emphasis on the word "consciously"), the spiritual warrior goes farther with less effort. As Bruce Lee put it: "The less effort, the faster and more powerful you will be."

Like many other people I knew of my generation, I also got turned on to the idea of the spiritual warrior through author Carlos Castaneda, an anthropologist who wrote *The Teachings of Don Juan*. This account of a psychedelic journey of self-discovery with a spiritual warrior/shaman blew our minds and went on to sell millions of copies. Castaneda was like Bruce Lee's spiritual brother. "Warriors do not win victories by beating their heads against walls, but by overtaking the walls," he wrote. "Warriors jump over walls, they don't demolish them."[48] Sisyphus represents the extremes, and the spiritual warrior walks the middle path. This is right effort.

As I continued my practice of mindfulness, I eventually realized that I was making things way too complicated, expending too much energy and wrong effort. I slowly became able to observe this attitude of mine. I learned to "be still and know," to let mindfulness and wisdom do the work, and just sit back and watch, wait, and learn.

With time, I shifted my perspective from that of the lone warrior to the spiritual warrior. I lived experientially what Ashin Tejaniya once wrote in *Awareness Alone Is Not Enough: Questions and Answers with Ashin Tejaniya*, "It is only when mindfulness and wisdom (clearly knowing) are continuous, where we see the beginning, middle and end, will we understand the true nature of the mind and body. As a result of continuous consistent practice from moment to moment." [49]

FOUR ASPECTS OF RIGHT EFFORT

The Buddha identified the following four aspects of right effort:

1. Guarding against unwholesome qualities arising that have heretofore not arisen

2. Observing and abandoning unwholesome qualities that have already arisen, rather than reacting to them

3. Developing new wholesome qualities

4. Sustaining wholesome qualities that currently exist

When you're directing your energy and effort in alignment with wholesome thoughts and feelings, you're practicing right effort. By wholesome thoughts and feelings, I mean qualities like lovingkindness, compassion, generosity, joy, gratitude, and openness.

On the other hand, if the intention behind your actions and efforts is motived by unwholesome thoughts—by unwholesome I mean fear, greed, anger, resentment, guilt, or other qualities associated with the hindrances and the negative wolves we tend to feed—then you're practicing wrong effort. Your mind is clouded with distractions and your emotions are roiled by longing, aversion, or agitation. All of this clouds your vision and impedes your game and your ability to get into the Zone.

WALKING THE TALK

One way of looking at right effort is to consider it as the expression of mindfulness in the realm of action. It's as much about cultivating and sustaining positive mind-states as it is about becoming aware of and abandoning unwholesome ones.

For example, love is a powerful emotion. When we labor for what we love and we love what we labor for, love and labor become one. The Beatles said it all in their song "All You Need Is Love." Jimi Hendrix was on to the same idea when he said, "When the power of love is greater than the love of power, we will know peace." The greatest commandment in the Bible is to love your neighbor as yourself.

Notice that the stiffest tree is most easily cracked, while the bamboo or willow survives by bending with the wind.[50]

—BRUCE LEE

Happiness is another positive mind-state that feeds right effort. In his book *The Happiness Advantage* Shawn Achor explores how the positive mind-state of happiness enhances our success, increases our cognitive functioning, and has an undoing effect on depression and anxiety.

Wherever you are on your path, right effort is the same: Joy is in the doing of the task and in the journey itself, however long or difficult. You move forward toward your goals, and you keep going. If you experience great resistance, you don't force or try to push a square peg into a round hole, and you don't keep pushing that boulder up the hill only to have it come back down on you. Instead, you get silent, focus, practice AOB to connect fully to the present moment, get clear on what's happening, change course, and get back on the right track.

Employing right effort is not always easy. In fact, it can be hard, because paying attention is hard. It often seems like our minds are hardwired to avoid being in the present moment at all costs, flitting around and being everywhere but right here, right now. As Jack Kornfield puts it, right effort is tough because we often don't want to see what's in the present moment. Says Kornfield: "You know, this idea of 'Be Here Now,' and so forth, it sounds good. It's not so good. It isn't, because what happens when you're here now? Has anybody looked? Pain, boredom, fear, loneliness, pleasure, joy, beautiful sunsets, wonderful tastes, horrible experiences, people being born, people dying, light, dark, up, down, parking your car on the wrong side of the street, getting your car towed; all those things. For if you live here, it means that you have to be open to what Zorba called 'The whole catastrophe.' Sometimes we don't want that. Right effort is the effort to see clearly."[51]

Making the effort to see clearly means that you're poised and take responsibility for what you see. This sustains right effort and walking your talk in the world. There's no way around this. I know a guy who worked hard and who was really committed to his work of robbing banks. That's obviously not right effort. Neither are short cuts, such as getting jacked up on steroids to enhance your performance; this is clearly "wrong" effort. Taking your aggression out on an opponent instead of cleaning up the anger in your own emotional house is also wrong effort.

Look at it this way: You can't preach the gospel in church and leave it at the pew. You can't practice being mindful on retreat or in touch with your spirituality in the sanctuary, and then go out into the world and not live according to spiritual or mindful principles in your encounters with family, friends, coworkers, and in society. In other words, don't think you can expect to live unwisely and think unwholesome thoughts, and then play a good game in life—whether you're playing that game on the soccer field or in a grocery store parking lot. You have to truly walk the talk; that is an expression of right effort.

As Sharon Salzberg put it in *Lovingkindness*, "We must stop fragmenting our lives. Telling lies at work and then expecting great truths in meditation is nonsensical. Using our sexual energy in a way that harms ourselves or others, and then expecting to know transcendent love in another arena, is mindless. Every aspect of our lives is connected to every other aspect of our lives. This truth is the basis for an awakened life." [52] Author Anne Lamott summed it up differently in recounting one of her late father's most important life lessons: "Don't be an asshole." [53]

Of course, sometimes it's easier to stay attached to unwholesome patterns of thinking than it is to abandon unwholesome mind-states and replace them with positive ones. Why? Precisely because they're habits and patterns. Practicing forgiveness, changing a negative self-concept, letting go of anger, resentment, or judgments—these efforts aren't easy and often take us so far into discomfort zones when we would prefer the security of our familiar comfort zones, even if they don't serve us or are unhealthy. It's way easier and more "comfortable" to stew in anger and resentment, for example, than to practice forgiveness. But the former will keep you mired in unwholesome thoughts and feelings, while the latter will open the door to true transformation and make you strong. "Anyone can hold a grudge," Doe Zantamata wrote, "but it takes a person with character to forgive. When you forgive, you release yourself from a painful burden. Forgiveness doesn't mean what happened was okay, and it doesn't mean that person should still be welcome in your life. It just means that you have made peace with the pain, and are ready to let it go."[54] When we let go of unnecessary emotional baggage, we are, quite simply, freer on every level.

MAKING IT UP

Change involves risk and getting comfortable with the unknown—and the unknown can be scary. Very scary. When I talk about this with players, I often refer to a line in the film *Indiana Jones and the Raiders of the Lost Ark*, when the heroine asks, "What are we going to do now?" and Indiana Jones replies, "I don't know. I'm making this up as we go along."

Life is a lot like that. We really don't know what will happen from one moment to the next, so having an adventurous spirit and living in the mystery are helpful. So is keeping in mind that the unknown path is the path where we will grow and learn the most. In *The Places That Scare You*, Pema Chödrön describes the path of the *bodhisattva* warrior. Bodhisattva is a Sanskrit word describing a great compassionate being who helps others on the path of ending suffering. "A warrior accepts that we can never know what will happen to us next. We can try to control the uncontrollable by looking for security and predictability, always hoping to be comfortable and safe. But the truth is that we can never avoid uncertainty. This not knowing is part of the adventure, and it's also what makes us unafraid.... The central question of a warrior's training is not how we avoid uncertainty and fear but how we relate to discomfort. How do we practice with difficulty, with our emotions, with the unpredictable encounters of an ordinary day?" [55]

Approaching these daily difficulties as a challenge, rather than as a risk, is another aspect of right effort and another distinguishing feature of the spiritual warrior. To quote Castaneda, "The basic difference between an ordinary man and a warrior is that a warrior takes everything as a challenge while an ordinary man takes everything as a blessing or a curse." The trick, he suggests, is about what we emphasize. "We can either make ourselves miserable," he says, "or we make ourselves strong. The amount of work is the same." Replace "work" with "effort" and you have the same formula: Right effort makes us strong. Wrong effort keeps us miserable. It's our choice.

If we make the choice to walk the path of the spiritual warrior, we have to act. To use another line from a movie, this time from *Star Wars: Episode V, The Empire Strikes Back:* "Do...or do not. There is no try." The whole scene takes place when Luke Skywalker thinks that his X-Wing Starfighter is about to sink into a bog.

He starts to panic, and the scene unfolds like this:

Luke Skywalker: Oh, no! We'll never get it out now!

Yoda: So certain, are you? Always with you, it cannot be done. Hear you nothing that I say?

Luke: Master, moving stones around is one thing, but this is…totally different!

Yoda: No! No different! Only different in your mind. You must unlearn what you have learned.

Luke: All right, I'll give it a try.

Yoda: No! Try not. Do…or do not. There is no try.

What Yoda is essentially saying is that Luke needs to commit. You either move forward with intention, or you don't. There's no in-between. You do—or you do not. You keep your intentions good and strong. That is right effort—even if you fail.

When we apply mindfulness to our experience in daily life on and off the court, we're cultivating positive energy, which creates the spiritual power called wisdom. When we practice diligence, our efforts are steadfast, enthusiastic, and poised. When you have faith in yourself and confidence in your practice, you want to do the work of right effort and cultivate positive mind-states. This means learning how to make states of mind such as mindfulness, happiness, love, or compassion arise and manifest. It also means knowing how to handle unwholesome states of mind. For example, when anger arises, you understand how to let it go without pushing it away or trying to get rid of it, which in any case doesn't work. Instead, with right effort you actually *pay more attention to the anger* when it arises and take the time to be with it, breathe with it, and let it go without effort. By taking this deliberate action, you naturally generate a positive mind-state, no matter how angry you are. You can intentionally choose to bring positive mind-states into existence—and through right effort, you learn to sustain them. We do this by learning how to sit and enjoy sitting, without overly exerting ourselves or making it a chore. It doesn't have to be a struggle.

THE LOVE OF THE GAME

Right motivation is connected to right effort. It's motivation that comes from inside, not from external forces. It's important to ask yourself, "What do I really want?" Start by being aware of your feelings—sometimes we're not even aware that we have feelings! Investigating your feelings helps you to see your motivation more clearly, as well as to see whether it is right motivation or not.

For a team, that means moving away from a motivation such as "let's work together to destroy our opponents" to "let's work together and do this wonderful stuff we love and get into flow." Wanting to beat the other team, or to go faster or throw better than someone, can be a great initial motivation, but it will wear out quickly and eventually wear you down, because there's always someone else to beat. If you stay focused on tearing something down instead of building it up, you won't end up feeling great because you'll simply be consumed by hatred, anger, contempt, or other emotions that lead to distress.

Right effort and right motivation focus our energy on "we," not "me." Once we're clear on this and we can walk the talk, the team becomes, as Phil Jackson once said, like "five fingers on a hand." [56] This is the case for any kind of team, athletic or otherwise. It's all about bringing a certain positive quality of energy to the table in every area of our lives, no matter where we are or who we're with. The real question is this: Can you bring into your life, both on and off the court, the love of the game, the love of being present, the love of being all that you can be, the love of being of service, the love of taking your humanity to another level?

This is right effort, and it's the engine that drives the pursuit of excellence. When your actions are based on right effort, you cultivate an entirely different energy; rather than acting out of greed, or doing things strictly for yourself or from self-interest, you act for selfless reasons and thus generate more energy and opportunity for flow. Because as long as there's a self there, as long as your ego-mind is focused on *how* you're doing instead of *what* you're doing, you're operating out of self-consciousness. This mindset generates insecurity, takes you out of the present moment, and makes it more difficult to get in touch with that still and powerful center space between stimulus and response where, as Bruce Lee says, you can "be like water."

SCHOOL OF NO SWORD

Let me develop this idea of stepping away from your self by recalling that scene in the *Kung Fu* television series, in which Caine has achieved such a level of mastery in meditation and archery that he's able to forget himself and, with seemingly no effort, to become one with his bow and arrow, hitting his target with his eyes closed. (*The pole, the arrow, the bow are all one. Not many things. Not different things. One.*) Bruce Lee dramatized this same intuitive no-effort kind of action during a scene in the film *Enter the Dragon*, when he dupes and conquers an opponent with the "art of fighting without fighting."

This "art of fighting without fighting" is evident in ancient samurai culture and a school of martial arts practice called the No Sword School, which is based on a tale about a sixteenth century swordsman who was so highly accomplished that he never actually had to use a sword to defeat his enemies. Instead, he used intuition and a feel for flow that came from being fully in the present moment, which gave him an awareness of how to cultivate his mind and move his body to fight without fighting. He did this with no effort, no sword, and no self getting in the way. This is a quintessential expression of right effort.

The No Sword philosophy is about blending and flowing with what is. It is actually an ancient principle. We're not talking about waging mental warfare, crushing your opponent, or any variation on that theme. This is not about exhausting your energy in an attempt to exhaust your opponent or to conquer someone or something. That is not right effort. Right effort heightens energy, rather than depletes it. Through the practice of mindfulness, learning to know and trust yourself well enough to tap into a greater energy around yourself, you become one with any situation. There is no separation between you and the object in front of you, whether that is a ball, a racquet, or an opponent. You go with what *is*, and you redirect your energy as needed by bringing your awareness and attention fully to the present moment. If the river is flowing downstream, you flow with it, in the same direction, instead of swimming against it. This basic metaphysics of flow is all around us, every day: If you're driving your car and it starts to skid, you go with the flow of your car and drive in the direction of the skid, not against it. That's how you regain control, even if it seems paradoxical. You widen your peripheral field of vision and have more information available to you about where to move your body, versus narrowing your field of vision and limiting the scope of your performance as a result.

WATCHING THE CAT

The practice of mindfulness helps us cultivate the capacity to self-regulate. What is self-regulation? Here's a simple example: Animal trainers were able to train a German shepherd to sit quietly and watch a cat walk by without pouncing on it. That means they were able to transform the dog's hardwired instinctual response through conditioning so that it can self-regulate its own response. This is no simple feat, since the dog's instinctive habitual response is to instantaneously go after that cat as fast as it can.

Self-regulation is closely connected with the power of self-efficacy. When you're faced with a challenge, do you have the mental suppleness and belief in yourself to get quiet, stay connected to that space between stimulus and response, and move forward with right effort? Or do you struggle against the challenge and ultimately give up because the negative self-talk and conditioning in your mind compels you to do so? Remember, the mind is likely to give up before the body does.

Now, if a dog can learn to self-regulate, then surely we can work through our own habitual patterns with the help of mindfulness. Many of us have obsessions that flare up and re-inforce those old patterns. Addicts and substance abusers are often triggered to get high after seeing someone use drugs in a movie. The obsession to use comes over them because of what's called "operative conditioning." This is the autonomic response, otherwise known as the Pavlovian response, which makes it almost instinctive for them to get high when they see an image of other people getting high.

This works in a myriad of different ways, depending on what our trigger is. But this autonomic response is not just mental; it's also physiological. When an emotional trigger gets pulled, neurotransmitters are released that create the craving to use. By creating a space between stimulus (the sight of using) and response (actually getting high), the addict can choose to respond and act differently. The physiological response shifts and the mental obsession dissipates. In a high-stress athletic event, the ability to react to another player's action without emotional triggers is often the difference between a wise decision and one that loses the game.

Mindfulness—through relaxed receptivity, a standing back, a stepping aside—enhances a non-reactive posture that facilitates this de-conditioning, which is a form of right effort. In athletic performance, right effort is also enhanced by forethought, the way we think about and prepare for something before it happens. Forethought is another word for practice. During practice, we are able to learn new things and test out ideas. We aren't under any pressure, so there's time for exploration: What if I swung my racket this way instead of that? What if I kicked with this part of my foot, or bent my knee like this? I would estimate that about ten percent of what we learn as athletes happens during the performance, the game. The remaining ninety percent of what you learn as an athlete you learn by practicing. Practice is part faith because you often don't get the fireworks and positive reinforcement of performance and it's in large part self-regulation, the ability to keep at something without responding to the emotional triggers of "I'm bad at it" or "I don't want to do it" and having the consistency and commitment that are part of right effort.

Archery is not practiced solely for hitting the target; the swordsman does not wield the sword just for the sake of outdoing his opponent; the dancer does not dance just to perform certain rhythmical movements of the body. The mind first had to be attuned to the Unconscious.[57]

—DAISETZ SUZUKI

We know that things are going to change. We know that we're going to get old, that we're going to die one day. Life is impermanent. We know this intellectually even if we don't want to think about it. One of the benefits of self-regulation and right effort is the ability to live more fully the moments we have. We're more deeply aware of the impermanence of life, and as a result we're better able to *choose* how we're going to respond to things, rather than react in a thoughtless or habitual fashion. If something unexpected happens that throws us for a loop, we can freak out and say: "This should *not* be happening!" Or we can train ourselves to respond and go with the flow. You can't keep what's happening from happening. But you can choose how to respond. You can react and get the sympathetic nervous system riled up and flood your body with stress hormones that impede your game. Or you can sit back, breathe, observe what's happening, and respond to what *is*, rather than what you think should be, could have been, or was supposed to be. "Okay, so this is happening instead of that. Wow, well, I need to change course and find a new path out of this situation."

Again, this is like being fluid like water, not rigid like ice. It's about responding to the flow of life around us rather than reacting, because responding *facilitates* flow; reacting obstructs it. When you're driven or motivated to act out of fear, anger, or any other unwholesome thoughts or feelings that cloud your mind, you generally react with wrong effort. That ultimately messes with your performance. You need to step back and investigate your feelings, pay attention, and observe them in order to abandon them. Develop and sustain wholesome thoughts, keeping your purpose and intention in mind.

Scientists at Northwestern University studying "flow networks" found that the "best" soccer players, the ones who were most valuable to their team over time, were not the ones who were the fastest or had the best kicks, but those who had the best flow. Lionel Messi, one of the best players in the world who is particularly known for his smooth and easy flow, ranked right at the top. A related study of Dutch soccer players in the journal *Psychology of Sport and Exercise* in 2011 found a similar correlation between success and flow.

Right effort also concerns maintaining a balance between mind and body. That's why right effort is often compared to the strings of a well-tuned instrument. If the strings are too tight, they'll break. If the strings are too loose, you won't be able to make them sound. You need to find the middle way. When applied to practicing our skill set, the middle way means deliberate practice, not practicing too hard, not focusing on winning or defeating an enemy, or achieving fame and glory. You exercise right effort for the love and joy of the game. Without love and joy motivating your efforts, you're not practicing right effort.

FORGET YOURSELF

There is a paradox woven into right effort that is connected to the Zone or flow experience: Though I frequently speak of the virtue of knowing oneself, I often tell players that the best way to know yourself is to forget yourself. We need to cultivate a clear mind—and then we need to step away from our mind so that right effort can feel like no effort. We let go of self while maintaining control or mastery of self. Isn't that what the Zone is all about? I'm reminded of the 2010 Olympic men's snowboarding competition in Vancouver, when snowboarder Shaun White performed the first ever Double McTwist 1260. Also known as the "Tomahawk," this wildly difficult aerial maneuver consisted of two inverted head-over-heels flips performed while spinning three and a half times above a steep and icy snow-packed drop. It was one of the most difficult moves ever attempted in the history of snowboarding and secured White the gold medal, after he'd beaten his own previous record-breaking win.

Later, when asked what he was thinking during that moment, White replied: "At that point you're really not thinking, you're just letting it happen. It's a mixture of being completely focused, then slightly not caring." I can't think of a better description of the Zone.

EUREKA!

Of course, Zone experiences aren't always that spectacular. When you're in the Zone, whether you're Shaun White or a weekend warrior, you're beyond space, time, and self-consciousness. You perform without thinking, in a state of pure being, rather than a state of doing (even though you are doing). That's the principle behind what's called a Eureka moment, and history is filled with them: famous cases of people having slipped into a Zone state and then solving complex problems or finding answers that have led to scientific or artistic breakthroughs.

But we all have small Eureka moments all the time. We may be trying to figure something out and can't come up with a solution. Maybe we're trying to fix something and can't figure out how to go about it, or we're unclear about how to move forward in a problematic situation or relationship. We've thought about it from every angle and even overthought so much that we're stuck with paralysis by analysis. The more we mentally exert and push for an answer, the more the answer eludes us.

Then in frustration or fatigue, we throw in the towel and step away from whatever it is. We go for a walk, take a shower, go for a drive. We basically stop thinking about it, give our minds a rest, and forget about ourselves and the problem for a while. And then guess what happens? Suddenly in that moment of no-thought and letting go, the answer comes to us, seemingly out of the blue.

But does it really come from "out of the blue"? It seems like the answer comes from outside you, but it actually comes from *within*, because that's where it's always been. It's not until—after focused concentration—you forget your self that your subconscious mind can deliver the answer to you. And your subconscious lives in that quiet center that you tap into through the practice of mindfulness. The more you practice mindfulness, the more this process can happen, whether you're charging across a field or sitting at your desk trying to figure something out. It's only in practicing awareness on a different level that we get to know this part of ourselves. As the poet W. H. Auden put it: "The center that I cannot find is known to my unconscious mind."[58]

A MAGICAL KIND OF CONDITION

With regular practice, we can find that center that is known to our unconscious minds. This is one of the most wonderful benefits of mindfulness, what rower Craig Lambert referred to as that "magical kind of condition."

I'm reminded of an anecdote that Jack Kornfield once told about a young boy who, to his father's astonishment, became an expert at throwing a ball without any prompting from this father. The boy had committed countless hours to deliberate practice and error correction. He believed in himself, loved the game of ball-throwing, and intended to master it. When he finally did attain a level of mastery, the boy wasn't proud or overly triumphant. As Kornfield recounts in his book *The Eightfold Path for the Householder*, he was simply grateful and felt free. "It was never that he had his way with the ball," Kornfield said. "Rather through his undistracted, absolutely focused, un-selfconscious attention, the invisible laws of physics had their way with him. Through the total submission of himself to the invisible laws, he found both dominion and spontaneity which he rightfully experienced as true freedom and joy."[59]

Simultaneously experiencing dominion and spontaneity—isn't that what Shaun White was talking about when he described his Zone state of mind as "being completely focused, then slightly not caring"? It's in this paradoxical state of mind, when we're in conscious flow and connected to something more expansive than ourselves, that we can let go, just "let it happen," and put our faith and trust in those invisible laws. This, as Kornfield suggests in that anecdote, is when we rightfully experience true freedom and joy.

SUPERPOWER PRACTICE FOUR: RIGHT EFFORT

Walk your talk. Who you are in the world at large is what you bring to your sport. Every mindful moment off the courts, no matter how small, improves your game on the courts. And every mindful moment off the courts, no matter how small, is mental preparation for your game on the courts. There is no separation.

Keep a daily journal of how you respond to certain situations. This will cultivate self-awareness and mental strength.

Ask yourself:

What was the situation?

What thoughts were you aware of during the situation?

What feelings were you aware of during the situation?

What action if any did you take during or after the situation?

As you write about this situation now, what belief systems or paradigms do you think you were operating from?

TRUST: THE SPACE BETWEEN THE THOUGHTS

CHAPTER 6

I did not grow up particularly religious and had generally thought of faith as something that needed to be balanced with wisdom, bearing in mind that too much faith and not enough wisdom becomes blind faith, and not enough faith and too much wisdom becomes cynicism. There is a middle path here. My idea of faith was significantly challenged many decades ago when I went to that first AA meeting and was confronted with the first two steps of the Twelve Step program. The first step was to believe or have faith in a Power greater than myself. The second was to make the decision to turn my life over to that Power, to the care of God, as I understood the concept of God.

That last part gave me carte blanche to really explore my faith: Did I have a traditional faith in a traditional God? What is the so-called "Universe"? How do I summon that "Universe"? When Han Solo said, "May the force be with you"—what exactly was that force he was referring to?

"God" means different things to different people. In her book *Help, Thanks, Wow*, author Anne Lamott grapples to find words for "God" and "prayer" that don't push too many buttons. Lamott suggests that if "God" is too "triggering" for some people, perhaps God could be called "the force that is beyond our comprehension but that in our pain or supplication or relief we don't need to define or have proof of or any established contact with." She also suggests the term the Greeks used: "the Really Real."

In the end Lamott concedes that what we call this Power doesn't really matter, adding: "I know some ironic believers who call God Howard, as in 'Our Father, who art in Heaven, Howard be thy name.'" Well, why not? The point here is not to get bogged down by the word and focus more on our hearts. Lamott continues, "Let's just say prayer is communication from our hearts to…the animating energy of love we are sometimes bold enough to believe in; to something unimaginably big, and not us. We could call this force Not Me, and Not Preachers Onstage with a Choir of 800. Or for convenience sake we could just say 'God.'"[60]

That makes sense to me. We could use the word Atman, or Christ Consciousness, or Muhammad Consciousness, or the Big Self. We could call it "the masterpiece within each human being" or the "divine spark" as the Jewish philosopher Martin Buber calls it. In *The Way of Man: According to the Teachings of Hasidism*, Buber writes, "Thus, a divine spark lives in every thing and being, but each spark is enclosed by an isolating shell. Only man can liberate it and re-join it with the Origin: by holding holy converse with the thing and using it in a holy manner, that is, so that his intention in doing so remains directed toward God's transcendence. Thus the divine immanence emerges from the exile of the 'shells.'"[61]

Sounds a lot like the caterpillar and the chrysalis.

BUDDHA NATURE

Since I committed to the path of mindfulness, I call that inner divinity our Buddha nature. We all have it. The potential for awakening is already within all of us. It is not something we have to get from outside ourselves. I recall the title of Sheldon Kopp's book, *If You Meet the Buddha on the Road, Kill Him!* This suggests that if you find someone or something claiming to actually *be* the Buddha, or to be this Divinity, you might be looking at what's called a "false God." What you're looking for—that Buddha nature—can only be found by turning inward.

When I was on my knees in the bathroom at work, in the first days of my sobriety decades ago, praying to *Something* for help, I was essentially reaching out to that "force that is beyond our comprehension." I took a leap of faith, hoping that what I'll call the Universe would take care of me. I let my guard down and got out of my own way. And here's what changed: everything. Slowly but surely, I understood things that had eluded me for so long and I had a connection to belief that was experiential, not intellectual.

There are no atheists in a foxhole, the familiar expression goes. Usually, in times of extreme crisis, the first thing people do is let their guard down and ask for help from Somewhere or Something. That certainly described me in my very own personal foxhole. I have since come to understand that the real dilemma for most people has to do with feeling a lack of power in their lives. Seeking and connecting to a higher consciousness is the key to establishing a strong spiritual foundation, which lets us open to what is unfolding, to the unknown future as it comes one day at a time, to wherever we are, to whatever game we're playing. That is the ultimate form of empowerment.

In the book *Faith: Trusting Your Own Deepest Experience*, Sharon Salzberg writes, "Finding a spiritual refuge is a significant step on the journey of faith. A trustworthy refuge enables us to go against the misleading promises of an unexamined world, to move beyond conditioned attitudes and responses, to eschew superficial or heartless answers to our deepest questions." [62] It takes courage to do this, particularly when we have no faith—in ourselves, in the world or in anything bigger than ourselves. It requires a much different leap of faith.

Trust is another word for faith—trusting that we can open to the next unfolding, to the unknown moment, and be vulnerable even to experiencing unpleasant feelings. It takes courage to be vulnerable and it takes being vulnerable to trust. In his book *The Courage to Create*, Rollo May describes this particular kind of courage. "A chief characteristic of this courage is that it requires a centeredness within our own being, without which we would feel ourselves to be a vacuum." [63] He adds that the word courage comes from the same stem as the French word *coeur*, meaning "heart." "Thus," adds May, "just as one's heart, by pumping blood to one's arms, legs, and brain, enables all the other physical organs to function, so courage makes possible all psychological virtues."

The heart, I might add, is where we physically experience that universal power called love.

In *The Power of Myth*, Joseph Campbell also spoke of courage, and touched on what might be considered one of the credos of the spiritual warrior. "The conquest of the fear of death is the recovery of life's joy," wrote Campbell. "One can experience an unconditional affirmation of life only when one has accepted death, not as contrary to life but as an aspect of life. Life in its becoming is always shedding death, and on the point of death. The conquest of fear yields the courage of life. That is the cardinal initiation of every heroic adventure—fearlessness and achievement." [64]

The idea of a conquest or a journey that leads to fearlessness and achievement is the path of the spiritual warrior or the bodhisattva warrior, and it's inseparable from our acceptance of impermanence. We are born and we die. We are all joined in this inevitable universal cycle. People who are aware of the imminence of death are often the ones who commit themselves most wholeheartedly to life, aware of the preciousness of each moment. Many have a heightened sense of purpose and urgency. This is the "gift," if you will, of impermanence. In February 2015, upon learning that he had a terminal illness, acclaimed neurologist and writer Oliver Sacks wrote in an essay in the *New York Times*, "I have been able to see my life as if from a great altitude, as a sort of landscape, and with a deepening sense of connection to all its parts.... I feel intensely alive.... There is no time for anything inessential." [65]

What if we played the game of life on and off the courts with this perspective, sense of purpose, and feeling of exalted urgency every day?

I have learned that the cultivation of each of the Five Superpowers—mindfulness, concentration, insight, right effort, and faith—can bring us to that place, and that each one supports and feeds off the others. There is great synergy here: Faith feeds insight, effort feeds concentration, and so on. The whole is always greater than the sum of the individual parts.

The fifth spiritual superpower, faith, is about having confidence and being open to new ideas. Faith becomes conviction when you actually *see* and *experience* faith at work. This, in turn, motivates you to move forward and fosters a strong belief in self-efficacy; you believe that no matter what happens, you can handle it.

This is how I got into the practice of mindfulness. I began to feel more fully myself when I was present and compassionate with people and could see the divinity in them, rather than looking at people as "other." I began to feel more deeply connected to myself when I looked at people as not separate from me. This sensibility helped me to discern when I was coming from a place of divinity and when I was coming from a place of self-centered fear, or from some other mind-state. Becoming acquainted with how it feels to be in the present moment helped me have the spaciousness to step back and realize, "Okay, everything arises and everything passes away." Everything is impermanent. Can I be with what is Now, with the immediacy of my experience? Can I get to the point where I am able to experience unity between my thoughts and my actions? When this happens, I can make decisions based on a deeper commitment: a commitment to be present, to be myself, to try to experience more than my suffering. I make a commitment to let go of grasping so that I can stand firm when I feel myself slipping out of a mindful state, or away from my own Buddha nature.

In the winter of 1988, I returned to the University of Massachusetts at Amherst, my alma mater, to celebrate Dr. J. He had retired as a player from the NBA the previous year and the university had seen fit to retire his collegiate jersey.

As I watched the crowd gathering and listened to the speeches, it dawned on me that if J was retiring, I too would probably be already retired, or retiring soon, if I had fulfilled my dream of playing basketball in the NBA. Sitting there on the metal folding chair, watching my dear friend, I finally let go of the dream I'd forgotten I even had, but that had remained in the back of my mind. I could accept the fact that I would never play basketball in an NBA game.

If you want to find God, hang out in the space between your thoughts.

—ALAN COHEN

Never in my wildest dreams did I ever think I would make it to the NBA as a Sports Psychology Consultant/Personal and Organizational Development Consultant and that I would directly and indirectly be part of eight NBA Championship runs and many college basketball conference championships, and play a role in the success of numerous professional and amateur athletes of every age and sport.

My own athletic "pure performance" looks very different now than how I had imagined it would when I was playing basketball in high school. About thirty years ago, as I mentioned,

I began to practice tai chi, an ancient Chinese discipline based on slow, meditative, flowing movements that connect the mind and body and promote wellness in many different ways. Westerners often don't realize that this silent, fluid, and graceful practice is actually a martial art, but indeed, that's what it is. According to tai chi historian Marvin Smalheiser, some tai chi masters gained notoriety for defeating their opponents with internal energy and movements so subtle that both opponents and spectators were unable to see what happened when these masters brought their opponents to the ground. They did so effortlessly (or we could say they used right effort at a masterful level), demonstrating the tai chi idea that "four ounces can deflect a thousand pounds." In this way, a David can defeat a Goliath with just a small amount of well-directed energy.

Tai chi is related to qigong, an ancient discipline with roots in Chinese medicine, which is predicated on the notion that human beings are miniature versions of the universe. In this way, we are all comprised of the constant interaction of five elements (wood, fire, earth, metal, and water) that flow in an interrelated manner throughout our bodies. In fact, it is not unlike how Rollo May described the heart pumping blood to all of our organs so that we can live, or the way courage "makes possible all psychological virtues." The intrinsic energy, *qi*, directed through the movements of qigong or tai chi, travels or flows along meridians in the body, aligning mind and body and connecting us to a much larger sense of intelligent flow outside ourselves.

What's love got to do with it?

—TINA TURNER

The sense of flow in tai chi looks very different but feels very much like what I have experienced in other physical activities when I've been in the Zone. Even if we're moving as fast as our bodies can possibly go in our sport of choice, we can tap into that same energy that flows around us in the slowly unfolding grace of tai chi. This energetic experience unites and transcends body and mind; it encompasses every thing and every one—much like the energetic power of love and joy. This experience can be very powerful. Bill Russell described his own Zone experience, saying he had "chills pulsing up and down my spine" and felt "as free and high as a sky hawk." And recall the rower Craig Lambert who called his flow experience "that magical kind of condition" when effort seems to disappear and there is no sense of a separate self. Lambert suggested that when you are in this special state, you experience "an expansion of consciousness" and the sense of being "on the path of spiritual growth."

In fact, you *are* on a path of spiritual growth in these moments, or at least you are in touch with the spark of something deeply spiritual. When you slip into the Zone state, it's almost as if you catch a glimpse of this path of spiritual growth—until, that is, you veer away from it. Mindfulness cultivates a sort of self-correcting dynamic that puts us back on the path, much like those lane-keeping assist systems on new "intelligent cars" that, according to their promoters, drive "as if guided by an invisible force."

The more you practice mindfulness and the more often you access conscious flow, the more you feel that spirit of love. Because in some respects, the two are connected to that same big "Something." The more you feel that greater spirit of love, the less room there is for distraction. There is no room for concerns about being good enough or better than so-and-so, for all the concerns about what other people will think or say in the future, or for how you did or what happened in the past. There is no room for any negative self-talk and distracting chatter, or for feeding the wolves of your hindrances.

Instead, you are flooded with consciousness and are fully and wholly concentrated on the here and now. This is the experience every athlete has when he or she is fully in the Zone. Sometimes we call this "being on fire." All distractions are burned away. This is pure performance at its best. This, ultimately, is the path of the mindful athlete.

SUPERPOWER PRACTICE FIVE: TRUST

Pure performance is, ultimately, a leap of faith. What else can be let go? What else can you strip away? Do your diligence, your right effort, and then take that leap. Release control of the moment. Close your eyes. Go.

ACKNOWLEDGMENTS

The author would like to thank the people below, and those whose names I've probably unpardonably forgotten, for their wisdom, friendship, and support.

My Family:
Edye N. Merzer my love and life partner, mother and father Emma Mumford (deceased), and William Mumford (deceased). Siblings, William Mumford, Jr. (deceased), Pearl Hughes (deceased), John Mumford, Betty Jenkins, Barbara Tucker, Edith Hicks, Juanita Mumford, Evelina Mumford, Linda Wilson, Donald Mumford, Mary Trotman, and Gregory Mumford.

Relatives:
Maternal Grandmother Mary Taylor, Aunt Sister (deceased) and Uncle Joe Smoot, Rick Lanier (deceased), Martin Hughes, Dr. Piper Smith-Mumford, Dawn Kelley, Darren Kelley, Darryl Hilliard, Harry Wilson Jr., Lloyd Mumford, Rashad Wilson. Nieces and nephews (including great- and great-great-). Cousins and relations, Carol Merzer, Rudy Bacalieri, Joy Freedman, Gail Merzer Behrens, Phyllis Veigh (deceased), Maurice Veigh, Aaron Jacobs, Cathy Jacobs, and Bruce Jacobs.

Coaches and Staff:

Phil Jackson, Tex Winter, Jim Cleamons, Kurt Rambis, Chip Schaefer, Jack Leaman, Rick Pitino, Al Skinner, Tim O'Shea, Bill Coen, Ed Cooley, Pat Duquette, Bonzie Colson, Preston Murphy, Christopher M. Holmes, Cathy Inglese, Pam Borton, Erik Johnson, Milan Brown, Brion Dunlap, Kevin Robinson, Dan Englestad, Kevin Driscoll, Matt Fava, Richard M. Regan, Ralph Willard, Ed Kelly, Alison Foley, Andrea Leonard, Sherren Granese, Jennifer Finley, Katie Meier, Alana Eichman, Shannon Gordon, Steve Bushee, Steve Basiel, Donna Bennett, Dr. Steve Julius, Dr. Derek Suite, Dr. Tom Mitchell, Dr. Kevin Pallis, Dr. Kevin Cooper, Dr. Marc Saulnier, Dr. K.S. Tsay, Dard Miller, and Brian Townsend.

Friends:

Julius Erving, Michael Jordan, Scotty Pippen, Kobe Bryant, Shaquille O'Neal, Derek Fisher, Jack Kornfield, Trudy Goodman, Sharon Salzberg, Joseph Goldstein, Larry Rosenberg, Narayan Liebenson, Jon Kabat-Zinn, Saki Santorelli, Clarence Gaines Jr., Joan Borysenko, Robin Casarjian, Roland Lazenby, John Reed, Eddie Carle (deceased), Mark Campbell, Fred Zackon, Lucie McInnes, Judy Lane, Jimmy Lawson, Nikki Geannelis, Joseph Kappel, Bill Kennedy, Steve Hailey, Reggie Jackson, Laura Georges, Kia McNeill, Nancy Legan, Wayne Selden,

Zach Auguste, Kyle Casey, Max Breiter, Henry Donnellan, Jim Afremow, Maddy Klyne, Maria Gray, Peter Bucklin, Diana Kamila, Carol Lewis, Anne Soulet, Meg Chang, Larry Peltz, Nancy Riemer, Ferris Buck Urbanoski, Elana Rosenbaum, Pamela Erdmann, Florence Meleo-Meyer, and Anne Skillings.

Prison Teachers and Staff:
Dennis Humphrey, James Egan, Chris Mitchell, Danielle Levi-Alvares, Eloisa Abislaiman, Catherine Chambers, Ellen Herman, Amy Lower, Greg Johnson, Stephanie P. Morgan, Troy Bell, Craig Smith, Sean Marshall, and Carolyn Mugar.

And last but not least my Publisher Parallax Press:
Rachel Neumann, Nancy Fish, Terry Barber, Terri Saul, Heather Harrison, and Jason Kim.

And special thanks to Debra Ollivier for her help with editing the book.

NOTES

1. Thich Nhat Hanh, *Being Peace* (Berkeley: Parallax Press, 2005).

2. Thich Nhat Hanh, *Old Path White Clouds* (Berkeley: Parallax Press, 1991).

3. Joseph Campbell, *Reflections on the Art of Living: A Joseph Campbell Companion* (New York: HarperCollins, 1991).

4. Joan Borysenko, *Guilt Is the Teacher, Love Is the Lesson* (New York: Grand Central Publishing, 1991).

5. Robert Frost, "A Servant to Servants" *Robert Frost: Early Poems*, ed. Robert Faggen (New York: Penguin, 1998).

6. Pema Chödrön, *The Places that Scare You: A Guide to Fearlessness in Difficult Times* (Boston: Shambhala Publications, 2001).

7. Joseph Campbell, *The Power of Myth* (New York: Anchor, 1991).

8. Sharon Salzberg, *Lovingkindness* (Boston: Shambhala Publications, 1995, 2002).

9. Jon Kabat-Zinn, *Wherever You Go There You Are* (New York: Hachette Books, 2005).

10. Daniel Smith, *Monkey Mind: A Memoir of Anxiety* (New York: Simon and Schuster, 2013).

11. Mihaly Csikszentmihalyi, "Go with the Flow" *Wired* magazine, September 1996. archive.wired.com/wired/archive/4.09/czik_pr.html

12. Mihaly Czikszentmihalyi, *Good Business: Leadership, Flow, and the Making of Meaning* (New York: Penguin, 2004).

13. William F. Russell, *Second Wind: The Memoirs of an Opinionated Man* (New York: Random House, 1979).

14. Craig Lambert, *Mind Over Water* (New York: Mariner Books, 1999).

15. Viktor Frankl, *Man's Search for Meaning* (Boston: Beacon Press, 2006).

16. Joseph Campbell, *The Power of Myth* (New York: Anchor, 1991).

17. Eckhart Tolle, *Stillness Speaks* (Novato, CA: New World Library, 2003).

18. Russell Simmons, *Do You! 12 Laws to Access the Power in You to Achieve Happiness and Success* (New York: Gotham, 2008).

19. Bruce Lee, *Tao of Jeet Kune Do* (Chicago: Black Belt Communications, 2011).

20. Sharon Salzberg, *Lovingkindness* (Boston: Shambhala Publications, 1995, 2002).

21. Bruce Lee, *Letters of the Dragon* (North Clarendon, VT: Tuttle Publishing, 1998).

22. Eugen Herrigel, *Zen in the Art of Archery* (New York: Vintage Books, 1999).

23. W. Timothy Gallwey and Zach Kleiman. *The Inner Game of Tennis: The Classic Guide to the Mental Side of Peak Performance* (New York: Random House, 1997).

24. Thich Nhat Hanh, *Present Moment Wonderful Moment* (Berkeley: Parallax Press, 2006).

25. Amit Ray, *Om Chanting and Meditation* (Rishikesh: Inner Light Publishers, 2010) and at: http://amitray.com/amitray_quotes/

26. Herbert Benson, and William Proctor *Relaxation Revolution: The Science and Genetics of Mind Body Healing* (New York: Scribner, 2011).

27. Cynthia Thatcher, "What Is Vipassana?" http://www.vipassanadhura.com/whatisvipassana.p.htm

28. http://www.jkrishnamurti.org/krishnamurti-teachings/view-text.php?tid=1015&chid=717

29. Mihaly Csikszentmihalyi, *Good Business* (New York: Penguin Books, 2004).

30. Timothy D. Wilson, *Strangers to Ourselves: The Adaptive Unconscious* (Cambridge MA: Bellknap Press, 2004).

31. Bruce Lee, *Tao of Jeet Kune Do* (Chicago: Black Belt Communications, 2011).

32. Ericsson, K. Anders, "The Role of Deliberate Practice in the Acquisition of Expert Performance." *Psychological Review*, 100(3), 363–406.

33. Malcolm Gladwell, *Outliers: The Story of Success* (New York: Back Bay Books, 2011).

34. http://www.newsweek.com/worlds-oldest-holocaust-survivor-alice-herz-sommer-dies-uk-230019

35. Jules Evans, *Philosophy for Life and Other Dangerous Situations* (Novato, CA: New World Library, 2013).

36. Pete Carroll, *Mindful* magazine. December 2014. http://www.mindful.org/mindful-magazine/the-game-changer

37. http://www.edgarcayce.org/are/edgarcayce.aspx?id=3558

38. Gunilla Norris, *Inviting Silence: Universal Principles of Meditation* (Katonah, NY: BlueBridge, 2004).

39. http://www.nimh.nih.gov/index.shtml

40. Hans Selye, *The Stress of Life* (New York: McGraw-Hill, 1978).

41. Wayne Dyer, *The Power of Intention: Learning to Ce-create Your World Your Way* (Carlsbad, CA: Hay House, 2005).

42. http://www.npr.org/2011/05/04/135985392/tavis-smiley-if-at-first-you-dont-succeed-fail-up

43. http://www.punnagai.com/wp-content/uploads/2012/09/inspiring-story-of-Soichiro-Honda.pdf

44. Neff, Kristen, *Self Compassion: The Proven Power of Being Kind to Yourself* (New York: William Morrow, 2011).

45. Robert Emmons, *Thanks! How Practicing Gratitude Can Make You Happier* (New York: Mariner Books, 2008).

46. https://www.psychologytoday.com/

47. http://bruceleefansite.com/quotes.html

48. Carlos Castaneda, *The Teachings of Don Juan: A Yaqui Way of Knowledge* (New York: Washington Square Press, 2011).

49. Sayadaw U. Tejaniya, *Awareness Alone Is Not Enough: Questions and Answers with Ashin Tejaniya* (Selangor, Malaysia: Auspicious Affinity, 2008).

50. http://www.bruceleequotes.org/

51. Jack Kornfield, *The Eightfold Path for the Householder: Ten Talks by Jack Kornfield.* http://www.buddhanet.net/pdf_file/ritepath.pdf

52. Sharon Salzberg, *Lovingkindness* (Boston: Shambhala Publications, 1995, 2002).

53. Anne Lamott, *Plan B: Further Thoughts on Faith* (New York: Riverhead, 2006).

54. Doe Zantamata, *Happiness in Your Life – Book One: Karma* (CreateSpace, 2012).

55. Pema Chödrön, *The Places That Scare You: A Guide to Fearlessness in Difficult Times* (Boston: Shambhala Publications, 2001).

56. http://www.cbssports.com/nba/writer/ken-berger/24796648/with-zingers-and-zen-phil-jackson-weighs-in-on-knicks-slow-start

57. Daisetz T. Suzuki in Eugen Herrigel, *Zen in the Art of Archery* (New York: Vintage Books, 1999).

58. W. H. Auden, "The Labyrinth." http://www.poemhunter.com/best-poems/wh-auden/the-labyrinth-2/

59. Jack Kornfield, *The Eightfold Path for the Householder* (DharmaNet, 1995).

60. Anne Lamott, *Help, Thanks, Wow* (New York: Riverhead, 2012).

61. Martin Buber, *The Way of Man According to the Teachings of Hasidism* (Bel Air, CA: Citadel, 2000).

62. Sharon Salzberg, *Faith: Trusting Your Own Deepest Experience* (New York: Riverhead, 2003).

63. Rollo May, *The Courage to Create* (New York: W.W. Norton & Company, 1994).

64. Joseph Campbell, *The Power of Myth* (New York: Anchor, 1991).

65. Oliver Sacks, "My Own Life" by ("Oliver Sacks on Learning He has Terminal Cancer") *New York Times* Feb. 19, 2015. http://www.nytimes.com/2015/02/19/opinion/oliver-sacks-on-learning-he-has-terminal-cancer.html?_r=0

BIBLIOGRAPHY

Achor, Shawn. *The Happiness Advantage: The seven Principles of Positive Psychology that Fuel Success and Performance at Work.* New York: Crown Business, 2010.

Batchelor, *Buddhism Without Beliefs: A Contemporary Guide to Awakening.* New York: Riverhead, 1998.

Carter, Rita. *Mapping the Mind.* Berkeley: UC Press, 2010.

Chopra, Deepak. *The Soul's Journey into the Mystery of Mysteries.* New York: Three Rivers Press, 2000.

Csikszentmihalyi, Mihaly. *Flow: The Psychology of Optimal Experience.* New York: Harper, 2008.

Deikman, Arthur J. *The Observing Self: Mysticism and Psychotherapy.* Boston: Beacon, 1983.

Evans, Jules. *Philosophy for Life and Other Dangerous Situations.* Novato, CA: New World Library, 2013.

Fromm, Erich. *The Art of Loving.* New York: Harper, 2006.

Gladwell, Malcolm. *Outliers: The Story of Success.* New York: Back Bay Books, 2011.

Goddard, Neville. *The Power of Awareness.* Textbook Classics, 2012.

Goldstein, Joseph, and Jack Kornfield. *Seeking the Heart of Wisdom: The Path of Insight Meditation.* Boston: Shambhala, 2001.

Hersey, Dr. Paul. *The Situational Leader.* New York: Warner Books, 1985.

Kabat-Zinn, Jon. *Full Catastrophe Living.* New York: Bantam, 2013.

———. *Mindfulness for Beginners.* Boulder: Sounds True, 2011.

———. *Wherever You Go There You Are.* New York: Hachette, 2005.

Kopp, Sheldon B. *If You Meet Buddha on the Road, Kill Him: The Pilgrimage of Psychotherapy Patients.* New York: Bantam, 1982.

Kornfield, Jack. *Meditation for Beginners.* Boulder: Sounds True, 2008.

Jackson, Phil. *Eleven Rings: The Soul of Success.* New York: Penguin, 2014.

———. *Sacred Hoops: Spiritual Lessons of a Hardwood Warrior.* New York: Hachette, 2006.

Lazenby, Roland. *Michael Jordan: The Life.* Roanoke, VA: Little, Brown, 2014.

Lencioni, Patrick. *The Five Dysfunctions of a Team: A Leadership Fable.* San Francisco: Jossey-Bass, 2002.

Lipton, Bruce H. *The Biology of Belief: Unleashing the Power of Consciousness, Matter, and Miracles.* Carlsbad, CA: Hay House, 2005.

Logan, Dave and John King. *Tribal Leadership: Leveraging Natural Groups to Build a Thriving Organization.* New York: Harper Business, 2011.

Nhat Hanh, Thich. *Being Peace*. Berkeley: Parallax Press, 2005.

Pema Chödrön. *The Places That Scare You: A Guide to Fearlessness in Difficult Times*. Boston: Shambhala, 2001.

———. *Start Where You Are*. Boston: Shambhala, 2001.

Ruiz, Don Miguel and Janet Mills. *The Four Agreements: A Practical Guide to Personal Freedom*. San Rafael, CA: Amber-Allen Publishing, 1997.

Russell, William F. *Second Wind: The Memoirs of an Opinionated Man*. New York: Random House, 1979.

Salzberg, Sharon. *Faith: Trusting Your Own Deepest Experience*. New York: Riverhead, 2003.

———. *Lovingkindness*. Boston: Shambhala, 2002.

Selye, Hans. *The Stress of Life*. New York: McGraw-Hill, 1978.

Simmons, Russell. *Do You! 12 Laws to Access the Power in You to Achieve Happiness and Success*. New York: Gotham (Penguin), 2008.

Smiley, Tavis. *Fail Up: 20 Lessons on Building Success from Failure*. Los Angeles: Smiley Books, 2013.

Watts, Alan. *The Wisdom of Insecurity: A Message for an Age of Anxiety*. New York: Vintage, 2011.

RELATED TITLES FROM PARALLAX PRESS

A Mindful Way, Jeanie Seward-Magee

Awakening Joy, James Baraz and Shoshana Alexander

Breathe, You Are Alive!, Thich Nhat Hanh

Buddha Mind Buddha Body, Thich Nhat Hanh

How to Sit, Thich Nhat Hanh

How to Walk, Thich Nhat Hanh

Love's Garden, Peggy Rowe-Ward and Larry Ward

Mindful Movements, Thich Nhat Hanh

Ten Breaths to Happiness, Glen Schneider

ABOUT THE AUTHOR

George Mumford has taught mindfulness and meditation since 1989, after he left his career as a financial planner and earned a Master's in counseling psychology. He worked at the University of Massachusetts Center for Mindfulness and directed a prison project that has taught mindfulness techniques to more than five thousand New England inmates.

While a student-athlete at the University of Massachusetts (where he roomed with Julius Erving), injuries forced Mumford out of basketball. The medications that relieved his pain also numbed him to the emptiness he felt without the game that had been his greatest passion—and led him to drugs. After getting clean and making meditation the center of his life, Mumford returned to the game he loves, teaching his revolutionary mindfulness techniques in the NBA.

When Michael Jordan left the Chicago Bulls to play baseball in 1993, the team was in crisis. Coach Phil Jackson, a long-time mindfulness practitioner, contacted Dr. Jon Kabat-Zinn to find someone who could teach mindfulness techniques to the struggling Bulls—someone who would have credibility and could speak the language of his players. Kabat-Zinn led Jackson to Mumford and their partnership began. George has worked with Phil Jackson and many of the NBA championship teams he coached.

He was also a part of the Boston College Eagles' legendary run from worst to first in the Big East alongside coach Al Skinner in 2001.

George Mumford teaches regularly at business and athletic conferences, nationally and internationally. He is currently part of Jackson's New York Knicks. He lives in Massachusetts.

**PARALLAX
PRESS**

Parallax Press, a nonprofit publisher founded by Zen Master Thich Nhat Hanh, publishes books and media on the art of mindful living and Engaged Buddhism. We are committed to offering teachings that help transform suffering and injustice. Our aspiration is to contribute to collective insight and awakening, bringing about a more joyful, healthy, and compassionate society.

For a copy of the catalog, please contact:

Parallax Press

P.O. Box 7355

Berkeley, CA

94707

parallax.org